D0479009

# CRAFTS
## FOR THE
# SPIRIT

# CRAFTS FOR THE SPIRIT

## 30 Beautiful Projects to Enhance Your Personal Journey

RONNI LUNDY

LARK BOOKS

A Division of Sterling Publishing Co., Inc.
New York

Dedication

To all the spirits
who brought me here.

Author: Ronni Lundy

Art Director: Dana Irwin

Photographer: Sandra Stambaugh

Interior and Cover Stylist: Dana Irwin

Cover Designer: Barbara Zaretsky

Illustrator: Olivier Rollin

Assistant Art Director: Hannes Charen

Assistant Editor: Nathalie Mornu

Production Assistance: Shannon Yokeley

Editorial Assistance: Delores Gosnell

## A Note About Suppliers

*Usually, the supplies you need for making the projects in Lark books can be found at your local craft supply store, discount mart, home improvement center, or retail shop relevant to the topic of the book. Occasionally, however, you may need to buy materials or tools from specialty suppliers. In order to provide you with the most up-to-date information, we have created a listing of suppliers on our Web site, which we update on a regular basis. Visit us at www.larkbooks.com, click on "Craft Supply Sources," and then click on the relevant topic. You will find numerous companies listed with their web address and/or mailing address and phone number.*

Library of Congress Cataloging-in-Publication Data

Lundy, Ronni.
  Crafts for the spirit : 30 beautiful projects to enhance your journey / Ronni Lundy.-- 1st ed.
      p. cm.
Includes index.
  ISBN 1-57990-412-2 (pbk.)
  1.  Handicraft. 2.  Spiritualism in art.  I. Title.
  TT157.L85 2003
  745.5--dc21
                                          2003004699

First Edition

Published by Lark Books, a division of
Sterling Publishing Co., Inc.
387 Park Avenue South, New York, N.Y. 10016

© 2003, Lark Books

Distributed in Canada by Sterling Publishing,
c/o Canadian Manda Group, One Atlantic Ave., Suite 105
Toronto, Ontario, Canada M6K 3E7

Distributed in the U.K. by Guild of Master Craftsman Publications Ltd.,
Castle Place, 166 High Street, Lewes, East Sussex, England
BN7 1XU
Tel: (+ 44) 1273 477374, Fax: (+ 44) 1273 478606, Email: pubs@thegmc-group.com, Web: www.gmcpublications.com

Distributed in Australia by Capricorn Link (Australia) Pty Ltd.,
P.O. Box 704, Windsor, NSW 2756 Australia

The written instructions, photographs, designs, patterns, and projects in this volume are intended for the personal use of the reader and may be reproduced for that purpose only. Any other use, especially commercial use, is forbidden under law without written permission of the copyright holder.

Every effort has been made to ensure that all the information in this book is accurate. However, due to differing conditions, tools, and individual skills, the publisher cannot be responsible for any injuries, losses, and other damages that may result from the use of the information in this book.

If you have questions or comments about this book, please contact:
Lark Books
67 Broadway
Asheville, NC 28801
(828) 253-0467
Manufactured in China

All rights reserved

ISBN: 1-57990-412-2

# Table Of Contents

# Introduction

Welcome to *Crafts for the Spirit*, a collection of some 30 projects to help you tend to your spirit. The dictionary defines spirit as "the animating principle of life, esp. of humans; vital essence." You don't need to subscribe to a specific belief to find peace or comfort in the objects here or in the rituals from which they come. You may simply make and use them with an open heart.

When we speak of the diversity of religions, we often focus on the differences between one belief system and another. But for all their differences, there is one thing that all religions and many philosophies share: the belief that each of us has within a soul or spirit that is connected to something larger, something mystical, something of grace.

Most faiths suggest that this spirit within yearns toward this larger entity, and agree that it is the primary work of the human here on earth to take care of that personal spirit in some way—to nurture it, protect it, and expand its awareness.

As each religion may differ in its concept of god or afterlife, so each has its own rituals or methods for such work. At one time, seekers of a larger spiritual knowledge were inclined to choose a single path and stay on it. But as our awareness of the world around us has expanded, so has our awareness of the many ways to care for our spirit. "The wood for a temple does not come from a single tree," one Chinese proverb says.

Contemporary seekers are as apt to discover meaningful rituals in several spiritual paths as they are to cleave to one. And we may also find it helpful to adapt those rituals to our personal needs and understandings in order to find a more powerful, genuine resonance with our spirit. This book is designed to introduce you to several ways of working with the spirit and caring for it, and to give you leeway to interpret those ways in a fashion that is suited to you.

Over the ages, humankind has developed many tools or objects to be used in expanding or caring for the spirit. They can be as esoteric as a Tibetan prayer flag or as ordinary as a painted pitcher for sipping color-energized water. They can range from a decorated pot for healing rituals to a simple mixture of scents for lifting the mood or opening the mind and heart.

Yes, you can buy many of these items ready-made. You may even be able to find genuine relics from ancient temples or foreign lands. But there is an immeasurable value in making a spirit object for yourself or for someone whose spirit you care for. And creating this object on your own terms allows you to think about and change the design in subtle ways that can have greater meaning for you. As Christian clergyman and newspaper editor Henry Ward Beecher once said, "Every artist dips his brush in his own soul, and paints his own nature into his pictures."

JON BOWER

Not all of the objects in this book are exact representations of something you might find if you were to visit, say, an ancient Celtic archaeological site, a Shinto temple or a mosque. In the introductions and sidebars that accompany these projects, you may find information about the culture it comes from and, when it is not rendered in the classic way, the traditional forms of the object may be depicted.

The designers have created these projects in ways that are respectful of tradition, but powerful or meaningful to each of them. And, when possible, you will find suggestions for ways in which you may easily and subtly change the object to suit your own spiritual need or orientation.

Most of the projects require neither elaborate tools nor particular craft expertise. In fact, a novice perspective may prove invaluable when working on these projects. As Sunryu Suzuki Roshi noted, "In the beginner's mind there are many possibilities, but in the expert's mind there are few."

So let the beginners begin.

# Getting Started

When doing any craft project, it is important to work in a comfortable, well-lighted, adequate space. Because of the nature of the projects in this book, you may want to consider some additional factors when choosing and setting up your work area, either temporary or permanent.

Many of the designers featured in this book have mentioned that the process of making the items on these pages can be an important part of your spiritual journey. Elisha Sigle, who tells how to make the beautiful zafus on page 74, notes that, "Sewing and beading are great times to chant or pray over your work of art."

Judi Ashe, whose stunning pottery is featured on the cover, teaches workshops in which the making of such objects is intended to heal the spirit. Of her work, Judi says, "It is truly my meditation to become silent and allow the language of my soul to come out through the clay."

Even work as simple as tracing and cutting the toran on page 103 can offer an opportunity to consider the deeper meanings of its paisley design and that of the *yin yang* symbol which inspired it.

To facilitate the contemplative aspect of creating your spirit craft, choose an area where you can work quietly, in solitude or with others working in a like-minded way. Give yourself physical space to spread out your materials and to work on your project, and also give yourself a generous amount of time for the work so you will not feel hurried in the process. ("Have patience," the ancient mystic Charan Singh advises. "In time, even grass becomes milk.") It can also be helpful to turn off phones and ask your family or housemates to respect your need to work without disturbance for a while.

> IT'S ALL RIGHT TO HAVE A GOOD TIME. THAT'S ONE OF THE MOST IMPORTANT MESSAGES OF ENLIGHTENMENT,
>
> *Thaddeus Golas*
> *The Lazy Man's Guide to Enlightenment*

SKIP WADE

You may want to perform a ritual of some sort to clarify your intentions while working. This could be as simple as saying aloud or writing on a piece of paper what you hope to learn or experience while making and using the object. Or you might want to follow the directions for smudging on page 40, or simply burn incense while you work to remind you of the intended spiritual nature of your craft project.

Quiet music can create an ideal background, both calming and lifting the spirit as you work. Many artists who create pieces with spiritual content place an object or picture in their work area, something to remind them of their connection to a greater power.

Before you begin, it is helpful to sit quietly for a few minutes in a relaxed posture and be mindful of your breathing. When you feel calm and centered, it is time to begin. The Sixth Century Chinese philosopher Lao Tzu said, "To the mind that is still, the whole universe surrenders."

While some skill may be helpful with certain pieces, the projects in this book were chosen because they can be crafted by anyone, including novices. Even the most skilled artisans make mistakes, however, and so it may be for you, as well. If something

doesn't turn out exactly as you have envisioned, you might consider the Japanese philosophy of *wabi-sabi* before you jettison it and begin again. *Wabi-sabi* translates as "the art of appreciating the imperfect." Those who practice it look for the deeper beauty to be observed in, say, a chipped vase housing a single spring flower; or an old, discarded table whose scratched and worn veneer and wobbly leg tells a rich story of usefulness and the passage of time. You may find it a surprising meditation to regard a flawed project through *wabi-sabi* eyes, perhaps discovering in it a greater beauty and deeper meaning than you had originally intended.

## TOOLS

The projects in this book feature a range of craft techniques including embroidery, paper cutting, pottery, beadwork, sewing, and others. Most of the projects can be made with tools and materials easily found in your home, or at craft and art supply stores. You will find a list of the items you need for a specific project with its instructions.

## DESIGN ELEMENTS

Because these projects have a spiritual intention, you may want to make or embellish them with colors, materials, or designs that have symbolic resonance for you. There are many books and Web sites where you can find information on the symbolism of specific belief systems or cultures. You can explore many

A *hare* or *rabbit* is thought to appear on the face of the moon in China and Japan, and likewise the moon is associated with this animal in both Celtic and Greco-Roman cultures, linking it to intuition, enchantment, and magic. (Hence the rabbit in the magician's hat?) But in many Christian cultures, it is a representation of lust. The Ojibwa of North America considered the hare to be the first teacher of plants and animals.

The *horse* is associated with indestructibility in Buddhism and represents purity and loyalty. In Northern European cultures, white horses were sacred and often used in rituals. In the Chinese Zodiac, it is the seventh animal and those born in its year are thought to be lucky with money.

The *cat* was revered and mummified in ancient Egypt, and perceived as a mother goddess who fiercely protected her young. But early Jews regarded cats as unclean, and they were feared by early Christians who associated them with witchcraft. The *manikineko* (an image of a cat with one upraised paw) is displayed in the windows of businesses throughout Japan because it is thought to bring prosperity. But they are despised among some Buddhists because, along with the snake, the cat did not cry at Buddha's death.

The *snake* plays the role of the tempter and the Devil in the Judeo-Christian creation, but in many other belief systems it is revered. Because it sheds its skin several times over the course of its life, the snake is often perceived as the symbol of transformation and change. In ancient China, this attribute made the snake a symbol of eternal life. The caduceus of Hermes, adopted as a symbol of the medical profession, is a staff with two snakes twined around it, representing death and regeneration. The snake biting its tail was a symbol of infinity in ancient Greece.

## CRYSTALS AND SEMI-PRECIOUS STONES

The use of crystals and gemstones for rituals has been common throughout time. Contemporary spiritual seekers often employ them for healing, meditation, energetic work, and balancing the chakras. When light is allowed to shine through a crystal, it is believed to spread the positive energy of the stone.

Here are some commonly used stones and the attributes associated with them.

*Agate* is perceived as a very powerful gemstone for healing because it is thought to stabilize energy and protect those who wear it. It is also thought to promote love and abundance. Moss agate, clear with a green moss-like hue, is thought to give strength, health, and wealth.

*Amethyst* of purple represents purity. Ancient Greeks and Romans thought amethyst could cure many incapacitating ills, such as drunkenness, infections, headaches, and cancers. Cups carved from amethyst were used for the process, as were amulets worn close to the skin. The stone is believed to balance and protect against sorcery and poison.

*Aquamarine* is thought to relieve anxiety and tension, leading to tranquility and peace of mind.

*Aventurine* is bright green quartz valued for promoting wellness in the circulatory, respiratory, muscular, and cardiovascular systems. Some African traditions say that the stone holds the power of the forest gods, so it was used to protect villages against evil.

*Carnelian* has been used in jewelry, seals, and sacred tablets by many cultures. An orange or dark red stone from central Africa, it is thought to bring joy and self-confidence and protect against blood disorders. If worn to bed, it can bring pleasant dreams.

*Hematite* is an iron ore commonly thought to have physical and metaphysical powers. Placed on the forehead, it is said to reduce fever, and is used to treat cramps, nerves, and insomnia. It is also believed to promote mental calm and help the wearer see her/his potential.

*Jade* worn as jewelry is believed to protect the wearer from injury and illness in certain Chinese traditions. The stone, which varies in color from bright green to white, is associated with serenity, vitality, and good health.

*Jasper* is mentioned in the Bible as a part of the Wall of Jerusalem, perhaps because of its association with health and rebirth, courage and calm.

*Lapis lazuli* looks like the night sky with its deep blue background and gold or silver flecks. Ancient Egyptians used it for scarabs to call down the protection of the heavens. It is associated with the divine feminine, and was often ground up and processed into ultramarine pigment used for the Virgin Mary's cloak in Renaissance paintings.

*Malachite* is first mentioned in a healing context in an Egyptian papyrus from 1600 BCE. It was used to heal asthma, arthritis, broken bones, toothaches, vertigo, and menstrual problems, and as an antidepressant and tension reliever. It is thought to protect against unexpected falls, but if it shatters, danger is foretold.

*Opal* is a multi-colored gem made of 30 percent water. Its malleable nature (warmth makes it more colorful when held in the hand; immersion in water renders it translucent) contributes to its reputation as a mystical stone, but also sometimes one of misfortune.

*Quartz crystal* is believed to be one of the first stones used as a talisman, as long ago as a million or more years. Because it looked like ice, ancient Greeks and Romans thought quartz had the power to quench thirst. It was a frequent fetish in many Native American cultures, used

for luck in hunting as well as in divination. Because of its clarity, it is believed to repel negative energy and attract positive, to aid in the diagnosis of illness and recharge the electromagnetic fields around the body. It is a symbol of balance and purity. Cylindrical crystals with two pointed ends are thought to be transmitters to and from the spirit world, while clustered crystals promote cooperation, fellowship, and friendship on the physical plane.

*Rose Quartz* is a peaceful delicate pink and is thought to promote calm.

*Tiger's Eye*, with orange, gold, and black striations of color, is believed to produce waves of soothing vibrations promoting self-confidence, calm, and understanding in difficult times, while preserving the fine balance between the *yin* and *yang* of the universe.

*Topaz* is commonly gold, but may be blue or other colors. All colors are thought to aid in peaceful dreams. Topaz symbolizes fidelity.

*Tourmaline*, like Joseph's coat, comes in many colors, and was used in many cultures for divination. Because of its multiple colors, tourmaline is believed to promote cooperation, understanding, and stability between opposing forces; it symbolizes hope.

*Turquoise* may be colored from deep green to pale greenish blue. The stone was sacred to the Toltecs and Aztecs and many southwestern Native Americans, particularly the Navajo. Pueblo tribes of New Mexico say the stone symbolizes not only the turquoise sky, which it seems to reflect, but the very breath of life and, hence, the spirit.

# Creating Sacred Space

The desire to set aside a particular space for reflection, prayer, or meditation is a timeless urge common to almost all spiritual paths. It is true that prayer and mindfulness can occur anywhere and at any time and that neither requires a sanctuary, but having a sacred space to retreat to can be an invaluable tool for kindling the fire within.

The area to be used should be set apart from the flow of daily life in the household. A small room or closet can be used if available, but simply designating a quiet corner for reflection is fine. A simple screen can be a useful tool in delineating such a space. Furnishings should be spare and not fussy: a chair or cush-ion to sit upon and a small table to hold an object of beauty and spiritual significance for focusing attention.

The object for focusing and meditation need not be expensive nor elaborate. North American poet Walt Whitman noted, "The morning glory at my window satisfies me more than the metaphysics of books." A century later, another great American writer, Henry Miller, said, "The moment one gives close attention to anything, even a blade of grass, it becomes a mysterious, awesome, indescribably magnificent world in itself."

This section contains several simple but beautiful craft projects to enable you to create a quiet space for contemplation that is uniquely your own.

IT IS AN EXCELLENT PLAN TO HAVE SOME PLACE WHERE WE CAN GO TO BE QUIET WHEN THINGS VEX OR GRIEVE US.

JON BOWER

THERE ARE A GOOD MANY HARD TIMES IN THIS LIFE
OF OURS,  BUT WE CAN ALWAYS BEAR THEM IF WE
ASK HELP IN THE RIGHT WAY.

*Louisa May Alcott*
*Little Women*

*Designer:* DIANA LIGHT

# DOORS OF PERCEPTION CURTAIN

Buddhist monasteries often feature entries with lowered lintels or raised thresholds to awaken your consciousness. This beaded curtain can be placed in the doorway to your private space at a height that requires you to just slightly bow your head as you enter or leave. It is a gentle reminder of the reflective work to be done in such a space. In addition, the pockets in the bead strands can hold objects or words representing things about which you wish to be mindful.

EVERY MORNING ZEN MASTER ZUIGAN WOULD SAY, "TODAY PLEASE TRY TO WAKE UP." THEN HE WOULD ANSWER HIMSELF, "YES, I WILL."

## MATERIALS

(Supply quantities will vary depending on the size curtain you make)

½-inch (1.5 cm) diameter wooden dowel, 3 feet (91.5 cm) long (or cut to fit snugly inside your doorjamb)

Silver acrylic spray paint

Plastic slide sleeves (20 square pockets to a sleeve)

3 sheets of tissue paper, each in a different shade of blue

2 sheets of vellum paper, one white, one plain blue or blue with tiny polka dots

3 mm metal eyelets or grommets

Decorative glass stones in several sizes and shades of blue

Silver-colored craft wire

20 feet (6.1 m) of small silver-colored chain cut into 8 pieces of various lengths

8 loose-leaf binder rings, ¾-inch (2 cm) in diameter

## TOOLS

Craft knife or scissors

Permanent marker in shade of blue that coordinates with tissue paper

Ruler

Single hole punch (optional)

Hammer

Metal-eyelet or grommet tool

Wire cutters

2 pairs of small pliers (at least one pair round-nosed)

## INSTRUCTIONS

### 1.

Coat the wooden dowel with silver spray paint, and set it aside to dry.

### 2.

Using the craft knife or scissors, cut the plastic slide sleeves into individual pockets, being careful to leave the side and bottom seals of each pocket intact. Cut as many pockets as you would like to include on your curtain.

### 3.

For each slide-sleeve pocket, cut a tissue paper square to fit inside. Slip a square into each pocket.

### 4.

Cut an equal number of squares from the sheets of vellum, making these about half the size of the tissue-paper squares.

### 5.

Trace a design representing love, peace, compassion, health, or something else you want to be conscious of during prayer or meditation onto each vellum square with the permanent blue marker. (We have used Japanese *kanji* in the sample project.) If you prefer, you can write words or wisdom sayings, or use cutout pictures to illustrate the papers. You can also slide small stones, pressed flowers, or other small objects that have meaning for you into the pocket.

### 6.

Insert metal eyelets into each slide-sleeve pocket, one at the top (the open end) and one at the bottom. To mark where the eyelets will go, measure ¼ inch (6 mm) down from the top and use the permanent marker to make a small mark, centered along the pocket's width, at this point. Measure $^1/4$ inch (6 mm) up from the bottom, and make a matching mark. Use the craft knife to cut a small X at each marked point.

### 7.

Pick one side of each sleeve to be the back. At the top end, use the single hole punch (or your craft knife) to cut a semi-circle that intersects the X on the back layer of the pocket only. This will allow you to slip the vellum squares in and out of the pockets, even after the eyelets have been inserted.

### 8.

Using the hammer and the eyelet tool, insert an eyelet into each hole.

### 9.

Slip a vellum square into each pocket.

### 10.

For each glass stone you plan to use on the curtain, cut a 3- to 4-inch (7.5 to 10 cm) length of craft wire. Use the pliers to wrap each stone in a length of wire, making a small curlicue or spiral at each end.

### 11.

Each length of chain will hold several stones and slide sleeve pockets; the number and location are up to you. Working with both pairs of pliers, simply open the chain links and hook a pocket or a stone onto the chain wherever you would like. Then use the pliers to close the links. If you have placed a stone at the end of a length, use the round-nosed pliers to tighten the spiral at its bottom, securing it in place.

### 12.

Thread the binder rings onto the dowel and suspend a length of chain from each one.

### 13.

Position the dowel snugly in the doorway so that you need to bow slightly to avoid hitting the center bead strands as you enter the space.

*Designer:* LUANN UDELL

# SIMPLE SHADE SCREEN

IT IS OFTEN IMPOSSIBLE TO SET ASIDE AN ENTIRE ROOM, EVEN A CLOSET, FOR CONTEMPLATION AND MEDITATION. BUT IT IS IMPORTANT TO HAVE A DESIGNATED SPACE FOR SUCH. THIS SIMPLE SCREEN MADE FROM A RICE PAPER WINDOW SHADE CAN BE HUNG IN A CORNER OF A QUIET ROOM TO INDICATE THE SPACE BEHIND IT IS FOR SPIRITUAL WORK. THE SCREEN CAN BE DECORATED WITH TORN PAPER SYMBOLS CHOSEN BY YOU FOR THEIR MEANING. THE SAMPLE SCREEN IS DECORATED WITH STARS AND THE SPIRAL, WHICH APPEARS FREQUENTLY AS A DESIGN MOTIF IN OCEANIC CULTURES, SYMBOLIZING CREATION FOR THE MAORI AND IMMORTALITY FOR POLYNESIANS.

THE MOST BEAUTIFUL THING WE CAN EXPERIENCE IS THE MYSTERIOUS. IT IS THE SOURCE OF ALL TRUE ART AND SCIENCE.

*Albert Einstein*
Physicist

## MATERIALS

Rice paper shade in desired size (Note: Many paper shades are now made of a synthetic fiber rather than real rice fiber, which doesn't make a good surface for gluing. Look for a shade that is made of real paper so that the collage pieces will adhere easily.)

Scrap paper

Several sheets of solid-colored, handmade papers

Permanent PVA archival glue

Clear fishing line or thin wire

Ceiling hooks or spring rod made for bath or curtains

## TOOLS

Soft pencil

Wide-tipped black marker

Small paintbrush

Jar of water

Old sheet (optional)

1-inch-wide (2.5 cm) flat paintbrush

Clean, damp rag

Small rubber brayer (optional)

## INSTRUCTIONS

### 1.

Sketch out some simple, broad shapes for the design on your shade. (The motifs in this project were enlarged from a set of rubber stamp images, so look around for a design that you like, or make up your own.) Draw each design in pencil on a separate sheet of scrap paper, then outline it with the black marker.

### 2.

To transfer each shape onto the colored paper, place it underneath the paper of your choice. (You should be able to see the bold outline of the shape underneath the paper.) Dip the small paintbrush in water, and follow the lines of the image as you trace it onto the handmade paper.

### 3.

Gently pull the handmade papers apart along the wet lines. (The paper should gently tear to create a soft, deck-led edge.) If the water dries before you finish tearing, simply retrace the image with the paintbrush. Paint and tear as many designs in various colors as you want for your hanging screen.

### 4.

Unroll the rice paper shade onto a large, flat work surface or onto a sheet spread out on the floor. If you don't want to use the roll-up hardware that comes on the shade, remove it, but leave the hanging hooks at the top of the shade.

**5.**

Position the torn-paper shapes in a pleasing pattern across the shade. If you're using a table, you may want to stand on a stepstool or chair for a better view of the whole shade while you decide where to place the shapes.

**6.**

Once you've placed the shapes, remove them one at a time from the shade to apply glue to them. To do this, place each shape on a sheet of scrap paper, and use the 1-inch (2.5 cm) flat paintbrush to gently brush a thin coat of glue onto the reverse side. Quickly place the shape, glue side down, in position on the screen. Keep the damp rag handy for wiping excess glue from your fingers so that they don't stick to the papers. When you're finished gluing, rinse and clean the flat paintbrush, leaving it slightly damp.

**7.**

Use the tips of your fingers to gently press and smooth each motif in place on the shade. Use the damp paintbrush to feather out the edges of each motif. (When the shapes are partially dry, follow up by smoothing them flat with a small brayer, if you wish.)

**8.**

Allow the screen to dry completely. To hang it, use the clear fishing line or thin wire to attach it to hooks in the ceiling or to a spring rod in a doorway or other opening.

SKIP WADE

WITH AN EYE
MADE QUIET BY
THE POWER
OF HARMONY,
AND THE DEEP
POWER OF JOY,
WE SEE INTO
THE LIFE OF
THINGS.

*William Wordsworth*
British poet

*Designer:* TERRY TAYLOR

# SMALL SHRINE

A SMALL SHRINE PLACED ON A SHELF, TABLE, OR IN A NICHE CREATES A FOCAL AREA FOR MEDITATION AND CONTEMPLATION. A ROCK, LEAF, ICON, PHOTOGRAPH, OR OTHER SIGNIFICANT SMALL OBJECT MAY BE PLACED ON THE SHRINE SPACE.

ARTIST VALENTIN GOMEZ CREATED THE SHRINE PICTURED IN THE BACKGROUND BY ROUTING OUT A PIECE OF 4-BY-4 LUMBER, A PROCESS THAT WAS ITSELF AN ACT OF DEDICATION AND CONTEMPLATION. DESIGNER TERRY TAYLOR CREATED THE PROJECT (FOREGROUND) AS A SIMPLER CONSTRUCTION FROM SMALL PIECES OF WOOD. YOU CAN DECORATE YOUR SHRINE WITH OBJECTS AND SYMBOLS THAT HAVE MEANING FOR YOU.

EVERY BELOVED OBJECT IS THE
CENTER POINT OF A PARADISE.

*Novalis*

German Romantic poet

## MATERIALS

Template opposite enlarged to scale

Craft box, approx. 6 inches square (15.2 cm)

Piece of basswood 40 inches long (1.2 m), and $^1/_2$ x $^1/_2$ inch in thickness and width (1.3 x 1.3 cm)

Piece of poplar or basswood approx. 12 inches long (30.5 cm), $^1/_4$ inch (6 mm) thick, and 6 inches wide (15.2 cm)

Wire nails $^1/_2$ x 19 (1.3 cm)

Flat-slotted brass wood screws 4 x $^5/_8$ inch (1.6 cm)

Craft wood decorative shapes of your choice

28-gauge copper sheet, 6 x 8 inches (15.2 x 20.3 cm)

36-gauge copper tooling foil

Copper foil tape

Wood glue

Sandpaper

Acrylic paints

## TOOLS

Pencil

Scissors

Hand jigsaw

Small motorized cutting tool and drill

Hammer

Screwdriver

Paintbrush

Ball peen hammer

Tin snips

Awl or small nail

Decorative craft punch

## INSTRUCTIONS

### 1.

Make two photocopies of the template opposite enlarged to scale. Adapt the template as you wish, adding a pointed roof, different front opening, and such. Cut out the templates.

### 2.

Cut four 10-inch lengths (25 cm) of the $^1/_2$ x $^1/_2$ inch (1.3 x 1.3 cm) basswood. Set them aside.

### 3.

Transfer the templates to the $^1/_4$ inch (6 mm) poplar or basswood board. Carefully cut out the shapes with a jigsaw or motorized cutting tool. Sand them lightly as needed. These two pieces are the front and back of the shrine.

### 4.

Measure and mark two 1 x 4-inch rectangles (2.5 x 10.2 cm) on the $^1/_2$ x $^1/_2$ inch (1.3 x 1.3 cm) basswood. Cut them out and sand them as needed.

### 5.

Nail and glue a 10-inch length (25 cm) of basswood from step 2 to each end of the 4-inch rectangles (10.2 cm). Line up the edges and ends of the long pieces with the edges of the rectangles. You've created two sides of the shrine. Set them aside.

### 6.

Nail and glue the front to the two side pieces. Turn the assembly over and nail the back to the assembly.

### 7.

Place the shrine assembly upright on the craft box. Mark around each "leg" of the shrine on the top of the box.

## 8.

Drill a small hole in the center of each marked square in step 7. Then, drill a small starter hole on the bottom of each leg.

## 9.

Use the small screws to attach the shrine legs to the box. Add a bit of wood glue before you tighten the screws.

## 10.

Glue any decorative wood shapes to the shrine.

## 11.

Paint the box and shrine with two or more coats of acrylic paint. Decorative painting techniques such as stenciling, sponging, and tole painting can be used to further adorn your shrine.

## 12.

Use the ball peen hammer to texture the copper sheet. Bend the sheet to fit the roof profile of your shrine. Trim the copper shape with the tin snips as needed.

## 13.

Pierce three or four small holes along two edges of the copper roof. Nail the roof to the shrine assembly with the wire nails.

## 14.

Using the leaf-shape craft punch, make copper leaves out of the tooling foil. Use a ballpoint pen to emboss the leaves with veins. Glue the leaves to the shrine.

## 15.

Adhere a strip of copper foil tape around the base of the box for decoration.

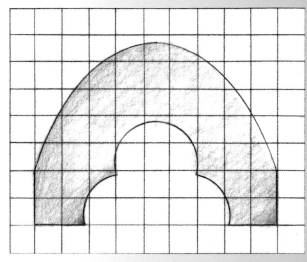

1 square = $^1/_2$ inch

*Designer:* TERRY TAYLOR

# RETABLO

THE CLASSIC RETABLO ON PAGE 33
WAS PAINTED BY ARTIST MARY JANE
MILLER ON METAL AND IS A REPRESENTA-
TION OF THE VIRGIN OF GUADALUPE,
REVERED THROUGHOUT MEXICO. IF YOU
ARE NOT HANDY WITH A PAINTBRUSH,
SIMPLY FOLLOW THE INSTRUCTIONS FOR
DESIGNER TERRY TAYLOR'S RETABLO OF
SAINT WALPURGIA, PICTURED HERE. TERRY
USED A COLOR PHOTOCOPY OF A BLACK
AND WHITE LINE DRAWING FROM AN OUT-
OF-PRINT COPY OF *LIVES OF THE SAINTS.*
THE COLOR COPY REPLICATES THE AGED
LOOK OF THE PAPER. CHOSE THE IMAGE
OF A HOLY PERSON OR TEACHER WHO
INSPIRES YOU.

AN OUNCE OF MOTHER IS WORTH A
POUND OF CLERGY.

Spanish proverb

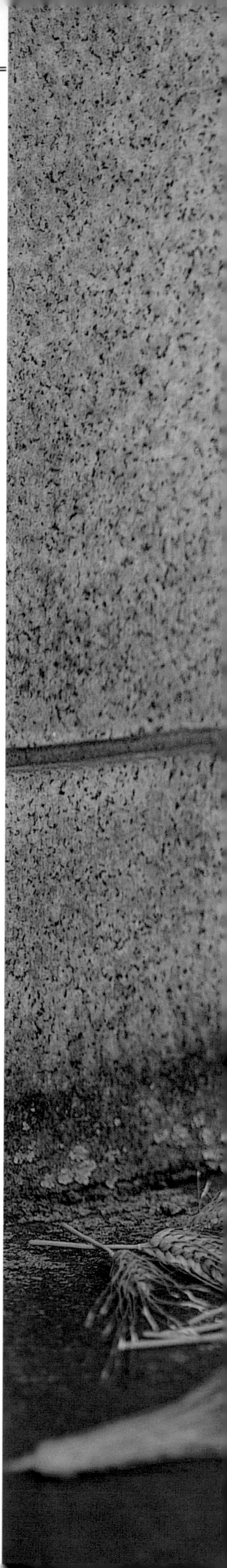

## MATERIALS

Photocopied image

Unfinished wood frame

Gold ink (optional)

1/4-inch-thick piece of basswood or plywood cut to fit inside frame

PVA glue

Wax paper

Crackle medium

Gold acrylic paint

Acrylic paint

## TOOLS

Fine-tipped paintbrush

Glue brush

Small paintbrush

## INSTRUCTIONS

### 1.

Make a color photocopy of the image you have chosen, sized to fit your frame opening.

### 2.

Use the gold ink to lightly accent any portion of the image that you desire.

### 3.

Spread an even coat of glue on the basswood. Lay the image on the wood. Carefully smooth out any wrinkles or air bubbles. Cover the image with a sheet of wax paper, weight it down with a heavy book, and allow it to dry overnight.

### 3.

Apply the crackle medium to the image, following the manufacturer's instructions. Apply acrylic paint as directed to highlight the crackle effect.

### 4.

Paint the frame as desired. If you're deft with a brush, you may wish to add a folk art pattern. The designer of this retablo chose a more subdued, modern touch.

# FAITH IS THE BIRD THAT FEELS THE LIGHT WHEN THE DAWN IS STILL DARK.

*Rabindranath Tagore*

Hindu sage

# *The* RETABLO

**R**etablos are a New World rendition of a Spanish Colonial religious art form. Without access to the same raw and manufactured materials that enabled European craftspeople to create elaborate icons, the new Catholic converts of the Americas made their own images of the saints out of what was at hand. These icons, still created today throughout Central and South America, and the southwestern United States, are painted on scrap tin or wood, and then mounted in a decorated frame.

The retablo may be placed in a niche or displayed on a table, and the area around it decorated with plants, food, milagros, beautiful fabrics, lovely beads or stones, and candles.

The intention is not to worship the icon or the saint represented on it. Instead it is thought that the presence of this altar in the home will bring good fortune to the inhabitants; and that the retablo and the area consecrated around it create a space that is conducive to prayer and contemplation.

*Designer:* JUDI ASHE

# SMUDGE POT

IN MANY CULTURES INCENSE OR SWEET-SMELLING HERBS ARE BURNED TO SANCTIFY A SPACE. THIS SAND-FILLED SMUDGE POT IS USED IN SUCH A RITUAL, DESCRIBED ON PAGE 40. WHEN NOT USED FOR SMUDGING, IT CAN SERVE AS A TINY ZEN ROCK GARDEN.

I DO NOT FEEL LIKE WRITING VERSES; BUT AS I LIGHT MY PERFUME-BURNER WITH MYRRH AND JASMINE INCENSE, THEY SUDDENLY BURGEON FROM MY HEART, LIKE FLOWERS IN A GARDEN.

*Hafiz*
Sufi sage

# PINCH POT INSTRUCTIONS

The description here for how to make a pinch pot should be used for making the Smudge Pot, the Hope Vessel (page 68), and the Purge Pot (page 106). Each was constructed out of raku clay, available at any clay supply store. Three pounds should be adequate for making a single pot. Very simple hand-building techniques are used, eliminating the need for a potter's wheel. Of the few tools used for these projects, most can be found in your own kitchen drawers.

These pots are sawdust fired in a simple backyard kiln which you can make (page 37). The kiln will hold several pots for a firing, so you may want to make all three projects within a matter of days, or gather together a small group of friends to each make a project, so you can fire multiple pots at one time.

The key to success with these pots is twofold: First, avoid making any joints in the pot. Second, dry the pieces for a long time—not hours, but many days—until they are bone dry, before sawdust firing them.

We suggest that you use a pinching technique to construct the pots. This is the first way pottery was made, and it is still very effective. The pots are formed out of a solid ball of clay that is pinched with the thumb and fingers to make a hollow vessel. The wall thickness should not exceed 3/8 inch (9.5 mm). Use your imagination and pinch a few practice pieces just to see what comes out.

You can also use a tool to form your vessel. Take a solid ball of clay and push a dowel or the end of a cooking spoon partway into it. Roll the ball as you rotate the dowel inside of it, slowly opening up the inside of the ball into a cone shape. This is a great way to get a good cone-shaped vessel. You can also use a potato that has been carved into a cone, and push it into the clay to create the

hollow vessel. Finish out the shape by working it between your fingers to thin the walls.

The Smudge Pot needs some legs to stand on, so leave some extra clay at the bottom and just pull it out into three small legs. Let it dry upside down for a while before putting weight on the legs. Or, make a little ring out of clay for the bottom of the pot to sit on.

The Hope Vessel and the Purge Pot both require a lid. Again, the pinch method works great. Also, you can use a round object such as an orange or grapefruit to shape the lid. Be sure to put a tissue or cheesecloth over the fruit before pressing the clay around it so that the clay will not stick to the fruit. You may want to pinch out a small handle when making the lid for the Hope Vessel, so leave some extra clay at the center top of the lid, and pull it out to form the handle.

The Purge Pot needs a depression in the lid deep and wide enough to accommodate a tea light candle. Wrap the candle in cheesecloth and use it to gently make the depression in the lid, widening it just a bit with your fingers when you have removed the candle.

You can apply various surface treatments to the outside of the pot to achieve different looks. You can impress the clay with wooden blocks or the end of a chopstick or knife, or press a shell or stone into it for texture.

Dry the pieces for many days. Make sure they are utterly dry before firing them. Fire them in the sawdust kiln (see opposite), then allow them to cool. Rinse them off gently in cool water and let dry. When they are rinsed and dried, you can apply acrylic paint to the outsides of the pots for some splashes of color, if you like.

The ritual for using the Smudge Pot is described on page 40; for the Hope Vessel, page 70; and for the Purge Pot, page 108.

*Designer:* JUDI ASHE

# LOW-FIRE KILN

*With this kiln you will be able to complete the projects presented on pages 34, 68, and 106.*

WE SHAPE CLAY INTO A POT, BUT IT IS THE EMPTINESS
INSIDE THAT HOLDS WHATEVER WE WANT.

*Tao Te Ching*

THE SMUDGE POT DESCRIBED HERE, THE PURGE POT ON PAGE 106, AND THE HOPE VESSEL ON PAGE 68 WERE ALL CREATED USING A BACKYARD, LOW-FIRE "KILN" MADE OF A METAL CAN DRILLED WITH HOLES AND FILLED WITH SAWDUST.

EACH FIRING IS DIFFERENT, AND THE RESULTS ARE COMPLETELY UNPREDICTABLE, WHICH IS THE BEAUTY OF IT. USING THIS TECHNIQUE, YOU CAN CREATE POTS THAT VARY FROM TOTALLY BLACK TO A MOTTLED SMOKY COLOR, WITH WONDERFUL MARKINGS FROM THE FIRE. AS A GENERAL GUIDE, THE FINER THE SAWDUST YOU USE, THE BLACKER THE POT WILL BE. ALSO,

HARDWOOD SAWDUST WILL PRODUCE A DARKER FINISH THAN OTHER WOODS. THE SAWDUST FIRING OF POTS IS AN ANCIENT TECHNIQUE, AND IS STILL PRACTICED TODAY BY MANY NATIVE CULTURES.

## MATERIALS

Old galvanized trashcan with a sturdy bottom and lid

Sawdust

Onion skins or banana peels (optional)

Newspaper

Matches

## TOOLS

Metal drill with 1/4 inch bit

# INSTRUCTIONS

### 1.

Drill holes spaced approximately 4 inches (10 cm) apart, all over the trashcan and on the bottom. Do not drill holes in the lid.

### 2.

Set the can up on blocks to allow ventilation from below. Place about 4 inches (10 cm) of sawdust in the bottom of the can. Gently place several pots on the layer of sawdust, allowing space between the pots. Put sawdust inside the pots too if you want coloration there. For additional surface coloration, you can throw in some onion skins or banana peels around the pots.

### 3.

Place approximately 2 inches ( 5 cm) of sawdust over the pots. Place your next layer of pots on top, continuing the process until you are near the top of the can. (You do not have to fill the can with pots if you have just a few.) Put about 3 inches (8 cm) of sawdust over the top of the last layer of pots, allowing about 4 inches (10 cm) of room on top of this for a layer of newspaper.

### 4.

Take three sheets of newspaper doubled over, twist and then bend them in half. Make enough of these twisted

### DESIGNER NOTE

*You can get sawdust at any cabinet-making shop or lumber supply that has a planer, or at a school that teaches woodshop classes. The sawdust should be medium-sized, and can be a mixture of hardwood and softwood. Sawdust from softwood burns much faster than sawdust from hardwoods.*

*Hardwood sawdust burns hotter and produces lots of carbon, creating the rich, black colors. The finer the sawdust, especially if it's hardwood, the longer it will take to fire, and the blacker the final colors will be on your pot.*

papers to cover the sawdust and fill the can. A generous amount of densely packed paper is required. Light the newspaper. When all the newspaper is burning, cover the can with the lid, and let everything smolder.

### 5.

Check to make sure that smoke is escaping through the holes you drilled, and crack the lid open if you need additional ventilation.

### 6.

The firing should take at least 12 hours. It is best if you can check the firing every few hours to make sure the sawdust is still smoldering. If it is not, you may need to fan the kiln to spark the fire again, or even make another layer of newspaper and light it. The longer you fire, the more carbon will go into your pots, causing a range of gray to black colors.

### 7.

Let the smoldering ashes cool before removing your pots from the bottom of the can.

JON BOWER

TO GIVE PLEASURE TO A SINGLE HEART BY
A SINGLE ACT IS BETTER THAN A
THOUSAND HEADS BOWING IN PRAYER.

*Mahatma Gandhi*

Indian spiritual leader

# *The Smudge Pot* RITUAL

by JUDI ASHE

The Smudge Pot is a tool for cleansing. It is derived from an ancient Native American tradition that involved the burning of sage or cedar or sweet grass to clear any negative energy from a room or from around a person. Now this ritual is often used as a way to set the tone for sacred or healing work. This smudging ritual can be done in a very simple way, or it can be part of an elaborate ceremony.

A smudge stick is a sheaf of herbs bound densely together so it will smolder when lit. You can find smudge sticks at health food stores, metaphysical bookstores, or other shops that sell items used in spiritual practices.

When the pot is fired and decorated, fill it with clean sand. You may "comb" the sand into a pleasing or significant pattern with a small pick comb, or a fork. You may want to place stones, beads, or other small objects in the sand. If you do, the pot can serve as a miniature contemplative garden as well.

When you are ready to smudge, take a moment to center yourself, become quiet, and breathe consciously. Some people feel that it helps to hold a prayer or intention in your mind and heart as you perform this ceremony. Hold the smudge stick over the smudge pot, which is filled with sand. Light the smudge and let it burn for a few seconds, then blow out the flame. The stick will continue to smolder, and a wonderfully aromatic smoke will rise up into the air. Simply move the smudge stick around the space, especially in the corners, and let the smoke do the work. It is not necessary to fill the room completely with smoke; a little bit goes a long way, and your smudge stick should last for many lightings. When you are finished, push the burning tip of the smudge stick down into the sand in the pot until it stops smoldering. It is suggested that a prayer of thanks or gratitude for this tool be used to end the ritual.

You can also smudge around your body or around someone else if you feel that negative energies may be lodged there. In this case, simply hold the intention again and move the smudge stick around the body, remembering to move it above the head and around the feet, as well as around each of the chakra centers.

You may also use the pot as a holder for burning incense as you meditate.

# WINDOW COLOR BAND

THE COLORS OF THE BEADS IN THIS BAND WERE CHOSEN FOR THEIR SUGGESTED HEALING PROPERTIES. THE BAND CAN BE HUNG IN A WINDOW OR NEXT TO ANOTHER LIGHT SOURCE SO THE RAYS SHINE THROUGH THOSE HUES. SOME COLOR THERAPISTS BELIEVE THAT THE ENERGY OF THESE COLORS WILL THEN BE TRANSFERRED TO THOSE WHO ARE IN THE PRESENCE OF THIS LIGHT. WHETHER THIS IS SO OR NOT, THE BEAUTY OF THE BAND CAN BRIGHTEN THE SPIRIT AND REMIND THE OBSERVER TO THINK HEALING THOUGHTS.

## MATERIALS

6 feet (1.8 m) of 16-gauge craft wire

7 large beads [can represent the 7 chakras (see page 11)], with holes large enough to string onto the wire and then also pass the beading needle through

10 grams of size 6 hexagon-shaped beads with holes large enough to string onto the wire

A variety of large and medium sized beads [can represent the 7 chakras]

Size D beading thread

## TOOLS

Round-nose pliers

Wire cutters

## INSTRUCTIONS

### 1.

Using the round-nose pliers, curl one end of the wire into a small circle, less than $1/4$ inch (6mm) in diameter.

### 2.

String the seven large beads onto the wire separated by three of the hexagon beads, including three hexagon beads at the beginning and end of the row.

### 3.

Cut the wire to $1/2$ inch (1.5 cm) beyond the last bead. Using the round-nose pliers, curl this remaining wire into a small circle, the same size as at the other end. Leave a little space at the end of the row of beads so you can get the needle and thread through the larger beads.

**4.**

Tie an 8-foot (2.5 m) length of thread to the wire next to the first or last large bead near the end of the wire. Thread the needle and pass through the large bead.

String beads in colors matching the large bead to the desired length, then string one hexagon bead. Skip the hexagon bead and pass the needle back through all the other beads.

**5.**

As shown in the illustration, pass the needle through the first large bead on the wire toward the other large beads on the wire. String three hexagon beads and pass through the next large bead on the wire.

**6.**

Repeat steps 5 and 6 for the other large beads, except for the last one. For that bead, work only step 5. Tie the thread securely in place and hide the remainder by weaving it back through the last strand of beads. Thread the needle with the remainder still hanging from the start of the beading, and hide it by weaving it into the beginning strand of beads.

**7.**

To make a loop for hanging, cut a 3-foot (91.5 cm) length of thread and tie it to the loop at one end of the wire, leaving a 6-inch (15 cm) tail. String a pattern of beads as shown in the photo, or choose any pattern you like. Pass through the other wire loop, and tie a knot. Pass the loose threads through the bead strands for 3 or 4 inches (between 7.5 and 10 cm), and cut close to the beads.

## *Color Band* RITUAL

One way to use the color band is to hang it in a window where the sun is shining. Sit in front of it so the light coming through will shine on you. Relax and close your eyes. Visualize the light coming through each strand of colored beads, one at a time, filling your body with that specific color's healing light. When you have imagined each of the colored lights, then imagine them blending together to form a full, golden light, and that light immersing your body with a feeling of harmony, balance, and wholeness.

LIFE IS A TRAIN OF MOODS LIKE A STRING OF BEADS, AND AS WE PASS THROUGH THEM THEY PROVE TO BE MANY COLORED LENSES.

*Ralph Waldo Emerson*
American transcendentalist

*Designer:* ANNE ASHLEY

# STAR LIGHT
*with*
# NINE POINTS

T HE STAR IS A UNIVERSAL
SYMBOL OF HOPE AND
ASPIRATION. THE NUMBER
NINE REPRESENTS THE POWER
OF THE TRIANGLE TRIPLED.
IN PYTHAGOREAN THEORY,
THE TRIANGLE REPRESENTS
PERFECT HARMONY, THE
COMING TOGETHER OF UNITY
AND DIVERSITY. OUR
NINE-POINTED STAR LIGHT
MADE OF PAPER CAN CREATE
AN AMBIANCE OF HOPE AND
HARMONY FOR YOUR SPECIAL
PLACE.

EARTH'S CRAMMED
WITH HEAVEN.

*Elizabeth Barrett Browning*
British poet

## MATERIALS

Star point pattern (see figure 1), enlarged to scale

1 sheet of poster board, thin cardboard, or matte board at least 14 inches (35.5 cm) square

3 sheets of colored paper, 18 x 24 inches (46 x 61 cm)

Materials to decorate with: rice paper, cloth, shaped hole punches, wallpaper

40-watt or lower-wattage light bulb

Light socket with cord and on/off switch

Decorative string or ribbon to wrap part of cord that is visible when lamp is hung

Glue

## TOOLS

Straightedge

Craft knife

Pencil with hard lead, such as 4H

Scissors

Hole punch

## INSTRUCTIONS

### 1.

Trace the enlarged pattern below onto the poster board. Use the straightedge and craft knife to carefully cut out the shape. This will become the template, making it easy to cut exact copies of the shape. Each shape folds to form one point of the star.

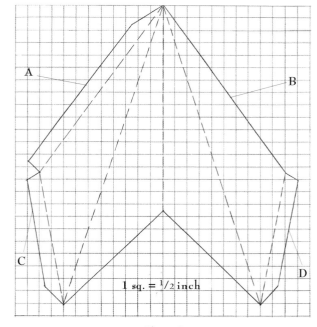

1 sq. = 1/2 inch

*Figure 1*

### 2.

Trace the template nine times on the colored paper (it should fit onto each sheet three times), and cut out the shapes.

### 3.

Decorate the shapes any way you like.

### 4.

As shown in figure 2, use the straightedge and pencil to draw lines for creasing on the back side of all the cutout

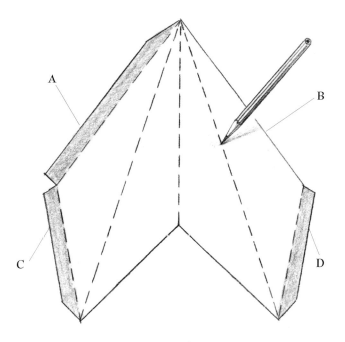

*Figure 2*

**8.**

Fold both sides of the top pattern piece in to meet in the middle. Apply a thin layer of glue to all of tab A. Press side B onto tab A, holding until the glue has set. Repeat with the remaining pattern pieces.

**9.**

While the star is still folded up, use the hole punch to randomly make holes in each segment.

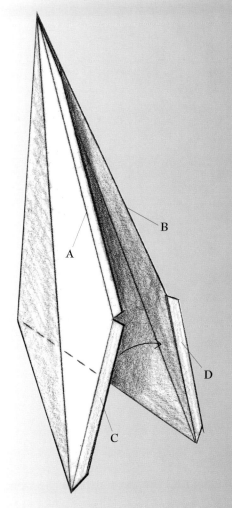

*Figure 3*

shapes of paper. The pencil slightly scores the paper for crisper folding.

**5.**

Fold along the score marks (excluding bottom tabs) of all nine pattern pieces, keeping the pencil line on the inside.

**6.**

Lay one pattern piece flat with tab A on the left side. Fold both sides to meet in the middle (figure 3). Apply a thin layer of glue to all of tab A. Press side B onto tab A, holding until the glue has set. The shape is flat now, but will become conical when the star is complete and opened.

**7.**

Apply glue to tabs C and D. Lay another pattern piece flat on top of the one you just glued, matching up the inner point and being careful to avoid the glue. Fold the tabs with glue up onto the second shape. Press and hold until the glue has set.

### 10.

On the top segment, punch two holes about 1 inch (2.5 cm) away from the inner point, one on each side of the center crease, as shown in figure 4. Thread a 6-inch (15 cm) length of ribbon or string through these holes, and tie. Flip the star over and do the same on the other side.

### 11.

Unfold the star. Place the lightbulb in the socket and put it inside the star (see figure 4). To keep the star open and the socket hidden, tie together the strings from step 10.

### 12.

Wrap decorative string or ribbon around the cord and hang it from a hook in the ceiling.

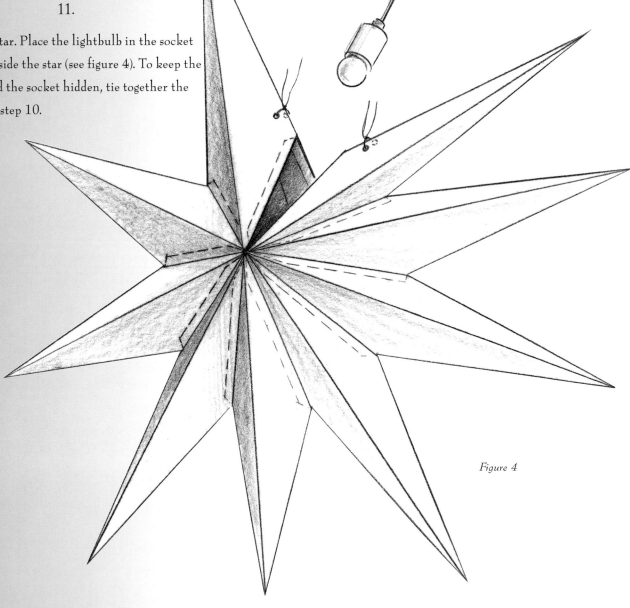

*Figure 4*

# THERE IS ONE RIVER OF TRUTH THAT RECEIVES TRIBUTARIES FROM EVERY SIDE.

*Clement of Alexandria*

early Christian theologian

DANA IRWIN

# LOOK AT EVERY PATH CLOSELY AND DELIBERATELY. TRY IT AS MANY TIMES AS YOU THINK NECESSARY. THEN ASK YOURSELF, AND YOURSELF ALONE, "DOES THIS PATH HAVE A HEART?" IF IT DOES, THE PATH IS GOOD; IF IT DOESN'T, IT IS OF NO USE.

*Don Juan*

Yaqui shaman

# The Journey Within

Meditation, contemplation, prayer, affirmation, study of wise words, or the wisdom of nature. There are many paths the seeker may take to centering and discovering the still small place within. Such a practice has value for those who use it as a means to enlightenment or simply as a method of calming the mind in daily life.

This chapter contains tools that can help you open the door to an inner understanding. It is up to you to fashion and use them in ways which resonate strongly for you.

JON BOWER

THE MOMENT AT WHICH YOU LOOK UP, THE MOMENT
AT WHICH YOU LOOK IN, STARTS THE JOURNEY BACK.

*Ram Dass*
American mystic

51

*The Journey Within*

*Designer:* TERRY TAYLOR

# TRAVEL ALTAR

A SACRED SPACE IN THE HOME CAN BE A BOON TO SPIRITUAL PRACTICE, BUT WHAT CAN YOU DO WHEN YOU TRAVEL? YOU CAN CREATE THIS TRAVEL ALTAR TO TAKE WITH YOU. THIS COLLECTION OF SMALL, SACRED OBJECTS ATTACHED TO A BOARD OR IN A CLOTH ROLL CAN BE PACKED AND CARRIED WITH YOU, ENABLING YOU TO CREATE A PERSONAL SACRED SPACE ANYWHERE YOU GO.

YOU CAN'T ALWAYS RETREAT FROM THE WORLD TO A COUNTRY HOUSE, THE SEASHORE OR THE MOUNTAINS. BUT IT IS ALWAYS IN YOUR POWER TO RETREAT INTO YOURSELF.

*Marcus Aurelius*
Roman emperor and philosopher

DESIGNER NOTE
The objects on these altars should
be chosen to spark reflection or
remind you of the precepts of
your particular faith. Mary Jane
Miller created what she calls a
Tiny Collection with *milagros*
sewn on a piece of old brocade
attached to a plain wooden board
(pictured here). It inspired Terry
Taylor to create the project (previous page), a felt roll in bright
colors echoing the strands of
marigolds found at Hindu shrines.
The metallic thread stitchery
combined with mirror tiles mim-
ics traditional Indian embroidery
in this portable shrine to Krishna,
one of the incarnations of Lord
Vishnu.

With the instructions that follow
you can adapt Terry's vision with
fabric and objects of your own
choosing, including beads, *kanji*
talismans, family pictures, feath-
ers or animal fetishes.

## MATERIALS

Amulets, holy medals, *milagros*, scapulars, etc.

Craft felt

Craft mirror tiles

Metallic embroidery thread

Ribbon

## TOOLS

Scissors

Craft punch

Decorative edge scissors

Sewing needle

## INSTRUCTIONS

### 1.

Select the amulets, medals or other objects that speak to you. Their size will determine the final size of the altar. Then choose colors of craft felt related to the divinity you are honoring.

### 2.

Cut out a central geometric shape on which to place the amulets. Use a craft punch to decorate the shape. This will allow the background color to peek through.

### 3.

Cut out two rectangles—one slightly larger than the other—to serve as the base of the altar. Use decorative edge scissors if desired.

### 4.

Use metallic embroidery thread to stitch the amulets to the geometric shape you created in step 2. Use large, straight stitches to applique the shape to the smaller of the two rectangles.

### 5.

Use a decorative punch to embellish the rectangle as desired.

### 6.

Small squares of felt serve as bases for the mirror tiles. Cut the felt slightly larger than the tile. Holding the tile on a felt square, stitch it to the rectangle with long, straight stitches.

### 7.

Sew the two rectangles together with a couple of rows of simple, straight stitching using metallic thread.

### 8.

Attach a short, folded length of ribbon to the back of the large rectangle to hang the altar.

*Designer:* NICOLE TUGGLE

# WISDOM BOOK

USE THIS BOOKLET TO RECORD PRAYERS, SPIRITUAL MEDITATIONS, WISE SAYINGS, AND PERSONAL PERCEPTIONS. ITS SMALL SIZE ALLOWS YOU TO DROP IT IN A COAT POCKET OR BAG SO IT IS ALWAYS CLOSE AT HAND. THE WORDS OF ZEN MASTER LIN-CHI MIGHT MAKE AN APPROPRIATE FIRST ENTRY: "TO STOP SIMPLY HANGING ON TO WHAT HAS BEEN IN THE PAST AND LONGING FOR WHAT MIGHT BE IN THE FUTURE IS BETTER THAN MAKING A TEN-YEAR PILGRIMAGE."

FOR THOSE WHO LOOK WITH THEIR PHYSICAL EYES, GOD IS NOWHERE TO BE SEEN. FOR THOSE WHO CONTEMPLATE GOD IN SPIRIT, GOD IS EVERYWHERE.

*Symeon*
Christian saint

### DESIGNER NOTE

*Muscovite mica, used as a visual embellishment over the image on the front of the book, also has symbolic import: it is said to increase understanding and perception and to enhance reflective abilities.*

## MATERIALS

8-12 sheets of text paper, each 12 x 4¹/₂ inches (30.5 x 11.5 cm)

10 inches of waxed linen thread or very thin ribbon

2 pieces of binder's board, each 6 x 5 inches (15 x 13 cm)

2 pieces of decorative cover paper, each 7 x 6 inches (18 x15 cm)

Piece of green paper, 5 x 4 inches (13 x 10 cm)

Piece of decorative text paper (dictionary, prayer sheet, *Bible* passage), 4¹/₂ x 3¹/₂ inches (11.5 x 9 cm)

Piece of beige paper, 3¹/₂ x 2¹/₂ inches (9 x 6.5 cm)

Small photocopy of symbolic image

Thin, transparent sheet of muscovite mica (available at gem stores or through similar on-line sources)

## TOOLS

Bone folder or dull butter knife

Ruler

Pencil

Awl or push pin

Needle

Clear-drying, archival craft glue

Brush for applying glue

Scissors

## INSTRUCTIONS

### 1.

Fold each of the text pages in half lengthwise. Press down along the folded edge with a bone folder or dull knife. Repeat until all the pages are ready. Slip one folded page inside another until all the sheets nest together like the pages of a book.

### 2.

Open the book at the middle and place it on a flat surface. Along the fold line, measure the center point, and poke a hole there with an awl or push pin, as shown in figure 1. Then make two more holes, one about 1 inch (2.5 cm) down from the top and the other the same distance from the bottom.

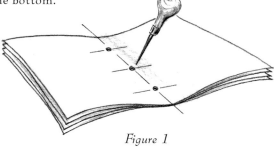

*Figure 1*

### 3.

Begin sewing the thread or ribbon through the pages starting from the inside center point. Leave a short tail of thread long enough to tie a knot later. (See figure 2.)

### 4.

Bring the thread to the top hole on the outside of the pages, and sew through again. Take the thread back through the center hole, to the outside, and down through the bottom hole.

### 5.

Bring the thread up to the thread tail at the center point, and tie off a knot. Trim off any excess thread. Set aside.

**6.**

Lay one piece of the decorative cover paper on a flat surface with the side you wish to have showing on the cover face down. Brush a thin layer of glue along one side of a cover board. Lay the board glue side down on the center of the decorative paper, leaving an even amount of paper along each edge. Press down. Flip the cover over and burnish the paper with a bone folder or dull knife, eliminating any air pockets and creating a smooth surface. Cut the edges of the cover paper according to figure 3. Glue down the edges. Repeat with the other cover. Allow to dry.

**7.**

Carefully brush a thin layer of glue across the top page of the sewn pages. You may need to put wax paper between it and the remaining pages to prevent them from getting stuck together. Place one of the cover boards, decorative paper side facing out, on top of the glued page, letting the text pages hang out from the left side 1/4 inch (6 mm). This will allow the book to open with ease. Use the bone folder or dull knife to burnish the text page along the inside of the cover, pushing out any air bubbles and making sure it is attached firmly. This text page is now the book's end paper. Repeat this same step with the back text page, adhering it to the back cover, letting the text pages hang out from the edge 1/4 inch (6 mm).

**8.**

Press the finished book under the weight of several heavy books or objects to ensure that the book will not warp and will dry flat.

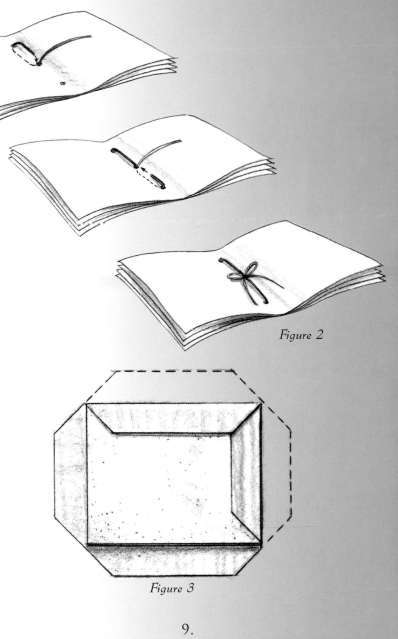

Figure 2

Figure 3

**9.**

For embellishment, simply glue down a series of decorative papers, starting with the largest first, adding the next smallest size on that. Here, we have used a dictionary excerpt with the definition of spirit, a small photocopy of a lotus flower, and a thin sheet of mica over the top.

*Designer:* ANNE ASHLEY

# WITNESS MIRROR

THE CONCEPT OF THE "STILL, SMALL VOICE WITHIN" OCCURS IN COUNTLESS DOCTRINES. MANY TEACH THAT THIS PRESENCE INSIDE IS A COMPASSIONATE OBSERVER THAT NEITHER PRAISES NOR CRITICIZES OUR ACTIONS, BUT SIMPLY ACCEPTS OUR JOURNEY WITH LOVE. MEDITATION IS ONE MEANS OF CONNECTING WITH THIS WITNESS WITHIN. ANOTHER METHOD IS TO GAZE DIRECTLY INTO YOUR OWN EYES IN A MIRROR UNTIL YOU FEEL YOU TRULY "SEE" INTO YOUR SOUL. SOME CONTEMPORARY THERAPISTS SUGGEST THAT YOU THEN SPEAK ALOUD TO FORGIVE YOURSELF AND TO ACCEPT WHO YOU ARE WITH LOVE AND COMPASSION AS THE FIRST STEP TO ACCEPTING OTHERS IN THE SAME WAY.

WE MUST NOT BE UNJUST AND REQUIRE FROM OURSELVES WHAT IS NOT IN OURSELVES. DO NOT DESIRE NOT TO BE WHAT YOU ARE, BUT DESIRE TO BE VERY WELL WHAT YOU ARE.

*St. Francis de Sales*
Sixteenth-century Catholic saint

## MATERIALS

Template (figure 1), enlarged to scale

Flexible board, 18 x 24 inches (46 x 61 cm)

Gold patterned rice paper, 18 x 24 inches (46 x 61 cm)

Blue patterned rice paper, 18 x 24 inches (46 x 61 cm)

Piece of mirror, 4 x 6 inches (10 x 15 cm)

Textured wallpaper, 2 x 27 inches (5 x 68.5 cm)

Green acrylic paint

4 small brass hinges

Small brass hasp

## TOOLS

Scissors

Pencil

Craft knife

Straightedge

Rubber cement with brush

Acid-free craft glue

Masking tape

## INSTRUCTIONS

### 1.

Cut out the enlarged template, and trace around it on the flexible board. Cut it out with the craft knife, using the straightedge to keep lines perfectly straight.

### 2.

Use the craft knife to lightly score the lines, as shown in the illustration. Fold along the scored lines and curve the top of the sides to close the arch.

### 3.

The box is easiest to decorate when it's unfolded, from back to front. Trace the template onto the gold rice paper; cut it out, adding approximately 1 inch (2.5 cm) of extra paper around its perimeter. Use rubber cement to attach the gold paper to the board. Fold the excess over the edges, and cement in place.

### 4.

Flip the board over. Trace the template onto the blue rice paper, and cut it out, following the line exactly. Use rubber cement to attach the blue paper to the board, making sure the shape fits crisply and covers the gold paper, but that it doesn't carry over to the other side.

### 5.

Refer to figure 2 for assembly. Use the acid-free craft glue to adhere the mirror to the blue rice paper in the center of the board, as marked on the template pattern. Make sure the edges match up with the side and bottom panels of the pattern.

**6.**

Fold up the box around the mirror. Curve the sides to fit, and glue them together, holding with masking tape until set. Remove the masking tape.

**7.**

Continue decorating by wrapping and gluing the textured wallpaper around the sides and bottom of the outside of the box. Paint the wallpaper the desired shade of green.

**8.**

Trace the doors of the pattern onto the blue rice paper. Cut out the shape, staying $1/2$ inch (1.5 cm) inside the line so that it's smaller than the door. Center the shape on the gold door, and glue. You can add other embellishments if you like, such as a strip of gold over the mirror or inside the door.

**9.**

Glue the hinges to the exterior of the box, 2 inches (5 cm) and 6 inches (15 cm) from the bottom. Glue the door hasp in the center, 4 inches (10 cm) from the bottom.

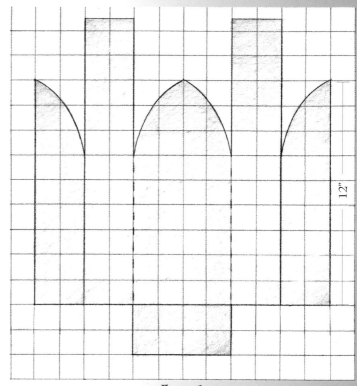

12"

Figure 1

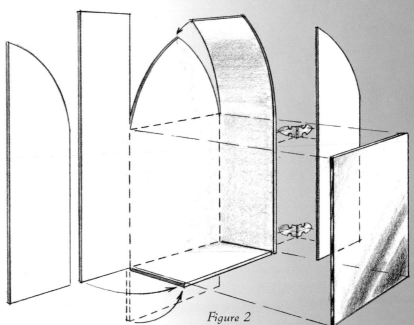

Figure 2

THERE COME TO US MOMENTS IN LIFE WHEN
ABOUT SOME THINGS WE NEED NO PROOF FROM
WITHOUT. A LITTLE VOICE WITHIN US TELLS US,

*Designer:* GABE CYR

# WITNESS PIN

However you choose to contact the still, small voice—your witness—during your times of contemplation, it is also helpful to make contact and listen to it while dealing with the stress of decisions and the perceived failures or disappointments of daily life. A talisman to remind you of your witness can be a useful tool. This witness pin can be worn over the heart to remind you to listen to your inner voice at any time.

## MATERIALS

Crafter's felt

Thread

Beads: seed, bugle, etc.

Beading thread

Suede, ultra-suede, or fake leather

Pin-back

## TOOLS

Pen

Sewing machine able to zigzag stitch

Beading needle

Scissors

Craft knife

Craft glue

"YOU ARE ON THE RIGHT TRACK, MOVE NEITHER TO YOUR LEFT NOR RIGHT, BUT KEEP TO THE STRAIGHT AND NARROW WAY."

*Mahatma Gandhi*
Indian spiritual leader

## INSTRUCTIONS

### 1.

On the felt, draw an oval outline that looks like a face. Sew over the drawn line with a very short, tight zigzag stitch that's about 1/8 inch (3 mm) wide. Cut out the face shape, leaving a 1/2-inch (1.5 cm) border outside the stitch line.

### 2.

Random bead two rows of beads just inside the zigzag stitching. To random bead, first pull beading thread from the back to the front of the felt, and string a few beads on the thread. Then hold the beads in place with your finger, drop the needle down through the felt, come back up behind the last bead, and then through it. You should anchor the line of beads every 1/2 inch (1.5 cm) or so, and more often in tight curves. (See figure 1.)

### 3.

Draw eyes, nose, and mouth on the face. Alternately, you could use a rubber stamp of a face. Bead these lines. Fill in the rest of the face with beads in colors that contrast with the beads you selected for the eyes, nose, and mouth. Don't worry about how the back of the felt looks, because it will be covered later.

### 4.

Cut away the felt outside the zigzag stitching. Place the face on the suede or leather-like material, trace and cut out. Place the suede on your work surface, so that the side you want to face out is facing up. Set the pin back on it, horizontally, in the upper third. Mark the positions of

*Figure 1*

both ends, and make a small vertical slit in the suede at each mark. You should be able to slide the locking mechanism and pin shank through from the top. Glue the pin-back to the suede. Set aside.

### 5.

You can make beaded hair for the pin by pulling thread through the felt in the appropriate spot, stringing a strand of beads, and bringing the needle back through the beads, starting with the one that's next to last. Or you can attach felted dreadlocks, yarn, wire, or raffia. The possibilities are wide open.

### 6.

To glue the beaded face to the suede back, first put glue on the back of the beaded face, staying 1/4 inch (6 mm) from the edge. Next put a line of glue on the pin-back, and press the suede to the back of the beaded face.

You can continue to embellish your pin by adding earrings, or beads in the hair.

THERE IS NOT A HEART BUT HAS ITS
MOMENTS OF LONGING, YEARNING
FOR SOMETHING BETTER, NOBLER,
HOLIER THAN IT KNOWS NOW.

*Henry Ward Beecher*
Nineteenth-century American clergyman

*Designer:* JUDI ASHE

# HOPE VESSEL

AFFIRMATIONS ARE ANOTHER WAY OF FINDING WHAT IT IS INSIDE OF US THAT SUSTAINS US, AND THEN MANIFESTING THAT SPIRIT OUTSIDE OF OURSELVES. THIS SIMPLE PINCH POT, FIRED IN A HOMEMADE SAWDUST KILN, ENABLES YOU TO CREATE A RITUAL FOR SUCH AFFIRMATIONS. INSTRUCTIONS FOR MAKING THE POT ARE ON PAGE 36 AND FOR THE KILN ARE ON PAGE 37. THE RITUAL FOR USING THE POT IS ON PAGE 70.

IF YOU WANT SOMETHING REALLY IMPORTANT TO BE DONE, YOU MUST NOT MERELY SATISFY THE REASON, YOU MUST MOVE THE HEART ALSO.

*Mahatma Gandhi*
Indian spiritual leader

*The Hope Vessel*
# RITUAL
BY JUDI ASHE

The Hope Vessel is a tool for manifesting your intentions. This ritual is based on the idea that we are co-creators with God, and that our intentions, hopes, and wishes do influence our reality in this physical plane. This ritual is wonderful when done in a group, but is also a powerful private ritual. Here are some suggestions for how to use the Hope Vessel.

Sit quietly and become centered. Reflect for a few moments about what things you would like to bring into your life. See them in your mind's eye as if they already exist. Feel them in your heart.

When you are ready, sit down in front of your Hope Vessel. Remove the lid. Have sitting nearby another bowl with some uncooked grains of rice in it. Gather a handful of rice into your hands. Focus your thoughts on one single intention while you hold the rice in your hands. Repeat the intention out loud or to yourself several times while you visualize the intention pouring out of your hands and into the grains of rice. Take your time with this and stay very focused. When you are finished, release the rice into the pot.

Do this for each intention. Store the "charged" rice in your Hope Vessel. When you have accumulated enough rice, say one cup, transfer it into a cooking pot, and prepare. When the rice is ready, become centered and quiet again.

Reflect upon each of your wishes as you eat your delicious "bowl of intentions." Believe that you have sent out a clear signal into the universe for these things to manifest in your life. Be mindful that this is a powerful ritual, so be careful what you ask for!

*Designer:* GABE CYR

# SACRED TEXT COVER

ALBERT EINSTEIN SAID: "THE MOST IMPORTANT FUNCTION OF SCIENCE IS TO AWAKEN THE COSMIC RELIGIOUS FEELING AND KEEP IT ALIVE."

FOR EINSTEIN, A SACRED TEXT MIGHT HAVE BEEN A BOOK ON PHYSICS. FOR OTHERS, IT MAY BE A TRANSLATION OF THE *BHAGHAVAD GITA*, THE *TAO TE CHING*, OR A BOOK OF PARTICULARLY MOVING POETRY. WORDS OF WISDOM CAN BE FOUND IN MANY PLACES, AND WHEN THEY ARE DISCOVERED, MANY SEEKERS FIND IT HELPFUL TO KEEP THE SPECIAL BOOK THAT CONTAINS THEM CLOSE AT HAND.

THE BIBLE IS LIKE A TELESCOPE. IF A MAN LOOKS THROUGH HIS TELESCOPE, THEN HE SEES WORLDS BEYOND; BUT IF HE LOOKS AT HIS TELESCOPE, THEN HE DOES NOT SEE ANYTHING BUT THAT.

*Phillips Brooks*
Bishop of Massachusetts, 1893

## B A S I C   B O O K   C O V E R

### MATERIALS

Fabric or flexible material to cover chosen book (amount
will vary depending on the book's size)

### TOOLS

Ruler

Pencil

Scissors

Glue, or needle and thread

Weight or clamp

### INSTRUCTIONS

#### 1.

Measure the height of the book, its width, and the distance around the book from cover edge to cover edge.

Add $3/4$ inch (2 cm) to the height measurement. Add the
width measurement plus 1 inch (2.5 cm) to the measurement from cover edge to cover edge.

#### 2.

This will give you the minimum dimensions of material
you need to cover your book. If the piece of material you
have chosen is larger, measure and cut to fit these dimensions. (See figure 1.)

#### 3.

Place the cover material on a work surface with the right
side facing down. Turn the side edges up $1/4$ inch (6 mm),
and sew or glue (see figure 2). If your cover is made of cloth,
use fabric glue and weight or clamp it until glue is set.

#### 4.

Turn the fabric over. Fold the cover around the book
evenly, with the wrong side facing out. On the outside of
the book cover, mark the top and bottom points where
the side edges inside the book meet with the outside.
Remove the book.

#### 5.

Place the cover material on a work surface with the right
side facing down. Turn the top and bottom edges up $1/4$
inch (6 mm), and sew or glue. (See figure 2.)

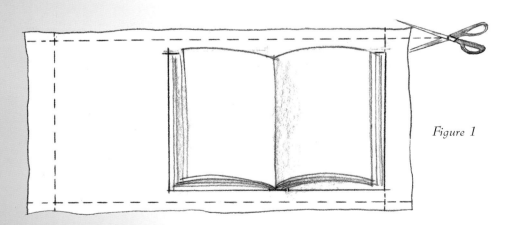

*Figure 1*

**6.**

With right sides together, fold the cover so that the side edges are aligned with the marks you made in step 4. Sew or glue the doubled edges, 1/4 inch (6 mm) from the top or bottom edges.

**7.**

Once a book cover has been crafted, you may choose painting, appliqué, embroidery, quilting, weaving, collage, handmade embellishments in ceramic or polymer clay, beads, natural materials, or even woodworking to decorate.

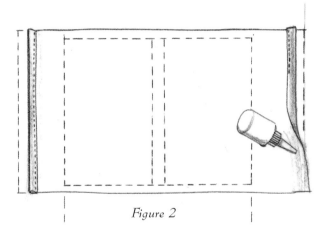

*Figure 2*

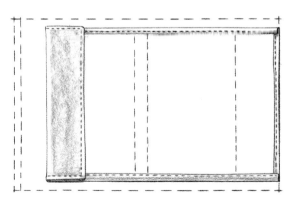

*Figure 3*

# BOOKMARK

If you like, you can create a permanent bookmark as part of your book cover.

## MATERIALS

Heavy thread, twine, ribbon, leather lacing, or similar material

Beads

## TOOLS

Ruler

Scissors

## INSTRUCTIONS

**1.**

Make a hole in the inner flap of the cover at the top.

Double the height of your book, and use this measurement to cut lengths of heavy thread, twine, ribbon, leather lacing, or other materials on which you can string beads.

**2.**

String through the hole in the cover, and knot all the strands together on either side of the hole.

Add beads to the ends of the strands, and make a knot to secure them.

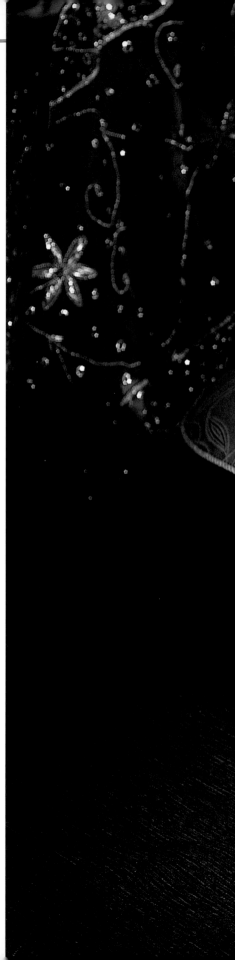

*Designer:* ELISHA SIGLE

# ZAFU

ZAFU IS A JAPANESE WORD FOR A SITTING CUSHION. YOU MAY FIND THAT MEDITATION IS EASIER WITH A COMFORTABLE ZAFU TO SIT ON. SEWING YOUR OWN CAN BE A CONTEMPLATIVE ACT IN ITSELF. DECORATE YOUR ZAFU WITH EMBROIDERY OR TALISMANS THAT HAVE MEANING FOR YOU ALONE.

ABIDE IN STILLNESS AND
YOU WILL EVENTUALLY
ENTER THE TRUE WAY.

*Tao te Ching*

## MATERIALS

Cardboard or heavy paper circle, 16 inches (40.5 cm) in diameter

$1/2$ yard (46 cm) of fabric for the top and bottom

Thread

3 yards (2.74 m) of edged twisted piping

6 inches (15 cm) of 54-inch-wide (1.37 m) fabric for the sides

Glass seed beads

Beading thread

Semiprecious gemstone, about 4 mm in diameter

4 pounds (1.8 kg) of stuffing material

Embroidery floss

## TOOLS

Scissors

Iron

Sewing machine

Beading needle

Chalk transfer pencil

Needle-nose pliers

Embroidery needle

## INSTRUCTIONS

### 1.

On the $1/2$ yard (46 cm) of fabric, trace the round template twice, and cut out the circles which will be the top and bottom of the zafu. Iron these, as well as the other fabric.

### 2.

Sew the piping to the top circle by laying it on the right side of the fabric, with the edging lined right up to the edge of the circle. Leave about 1 inch (2.5 cm) of piping at the beginning and at the end after overlapping the piping to close the circle before you cut it off. (Always lock your stitches by sewing backward $1/2$ inch (1.5 cm), and then cut the thread.) Repeat this procedure for the bottom circle.

### 3.

Flip the circles so the wrong side of the fabric faces up; you will see the stitches you just made. Following these stitches, sew right on top of them to attach the side piece. Do this by putting the right sides of the side piece together and either the top or bottom circle, lining up the long side of the side piece's edge with the edge of the circle fabric and sandwiching the piping. Start sewing at least $3/4$ inch (2 cm) from the beginning of the side piece, following the previous stitching. Do not overlap the edges, because that will make it harder to stuff the zafu. Leave 5 inches (13 cm) of excess material in the side fabric's length, cutting off the rest. Repeat this procedure with the other circle. Cut the extra side fabric to 2 inches (5 cm) and then turn the pillow right side out through the opening.

### 4.

Draw any simple single-lined symbol, for example an om symbol, onto the side fabric opposite the opening. Thread the beading needle with about 2 yards (1.8 m) of thread, double it, and tie a knot at the ends. Put one seed bead on, wrap the thread around the bead once, and come back through it. This prevents the knot from pulling through the fabric. Enter through the opening of the pillow, go to a good starting point on the symbol, and pull the needle to the outside. Begin with three or four beads on the thread. Lay them along the symbol, push the needle into the pillow where the line of beads stops, and pull it back up where the line of beads began. Go through the beads again. Repeat, beading the entire symbol.

### 5.

To smooth the beadwork, finish by connecting all the little groups of four beads. Start at one end and go through just the beads, not the fabric, all the way around the symbol. If it is hard to get the needle through the beads, use needle-nose pliers to pull it. If it seems a bead may break, skip it by sewing underneath to the next bead. Tie the final knot on the inside by grabbing a small piece of fabric with the needle, making a loop, sending your needle through the loop, and pulling tightly. Do this a couple of times, then cut the thread, leaving at least 1 inch (2.5 cm).

### 6.

If you did an om symbol, sew the gemstone dot on, going through it at least twice.

### 7.

To stuff your pillow, push the stuffing to the back and against the edging. Avoid lumping, and fill it as much as you can, always pushing toward the piping edges and the center. Hold the sides at the end of the stuffing so they won't tear. The sitting cushion should be extremely firm.

### 8.

Line up the edges of the side fabric to close the hole neatly, using three strands of embroidery floss threaded onto the needle.

### 9.

Clean off any fuzz, and sit on the cushion to shape it.

# Honoring the Body

Yoga, tai chi, and capoeira are all spiritual disciplines that approach strengthening the mind and soul by working with the body. But it's not only esoteric systems that preach about the mind/body connection. Contemporary psychotherapy continues to find links between a person's state of mind and her health; and there are increasingly intriguing new studies that suggest there can be beneficial physical effects from the practice of prayer, meditation, or active imaging exercises.

Gabrielle Roth, who teaches healing through movement and dance, notes that, "Everything that happens to you is stored and reflected in your body. The relationship of yourself to your body is indivisible, inescapable, unavoidable. In the marriage of flesh and spirit, divorce is impossible."

The projects here can be used to remind you of that connection and of the need to treat your body with the same respect you afford your soul.

JON BOWER

THE BODY, BEING THE TEMPLE OF THE LIVING
SPIRIT, SHOULD BE CAREFULLY TENDED IN ORDER
TO MAKE IT A PERFECT INSTRUMENT.

*Swami Vishnu-Devananda*

Twentieth-century yogi

*Honoring the Body*

*Designer:* JANE DAVIS

# CHAKRA BRACELETS

CARING FOR THE BODY DOESN'T NEED TO BE CONFINED TO THE SPECIFIC TIMES THAT WE EXERCISE. IT CAN BE AN INTERNALIZED PROCESS BY WHICH WE ARE MINDFUL OF OUR BREATHING, POSTURE, AND FLEXIBILITY THROUGHOUT THE DAY. THESE LOVELY BRACELETS CAN SERVE AS A VISUAL AND TACTILE STIMULUS TO PAY ATTENTION TO WHAT THE BODY IS SAYING TO US. USE STONES THAT REPRESENT THE SEVEN CHAKRAS TO REMIND YOURSELF OF THE NEED FOR BALANCE IN ALL ASPECTS OF YOUR LIFE. OR YOU CAN MAKE A BRACELET WITH JUST ONE-COLOR OF STONE TO HELP YOU FOCUS ON A PART OF YOUR CHAKRA ENERGY THAT NEEDS SUPPORT.

> BODY AND MIND HAVE A WONDERFUL RELATIONSHIP. THE ARRANGEMENT IS SUCH THAT IF ONE IS STABLE, THE OTHER IS STABLE. IF ONE IS HAPPY, THE OTHER IS HAPPY.

*Shyama Charan Lahiri*
Nineteenth-century yogi

## SMALL BRACELET

### MATERIALS

21 stones, 4 mm, 3 in each color representing each chakra

8 spacer beads, such as ¼-inch (6 mm) leaf beads

3 beads, ⅛ inch long (3 mm)

7 grams of size 11 seed beads

## LARGE BRACELET

### MATERIALS

7 stones, 8 mm, 1 in each color representing each chakra

8 spacer beads, such as 6 mm wide beads

4 size 8 gold-tone beads

10 grams of size 6 hexagon shaped beads

## BOTH BRACELETS

### TOOLS

Size 11 beading needle

Size D beading thread

Clasp

Clear fingernail polish or glue

## INSTRUCTIONS

### 1.

Tie a 6-foot (1.8 m) length of thread to one of the clasp components. Thread the needle and string the beads as in the project photo, or create your own design. String on the other part of the clasp component.

### 2.

Pass the needle and thread back through all the beads, and tie the working and tail thread together.

### 3.

Pass the thread back through about half of the beads, and cut it close to the beads. Thread the tail with the needle and pass that through the beads about halfway and cut it close to the beads.

### 4.

Put a small dab of the glue or fingernail polish on the thread knots to lock them in place, and let dry.

## *Symbolism of* COPPER

Although there is not much in the way of scientific evidence to support it, the belief that copper has healing powers has been prevalent for centuries. Copper bracelets are still worn today to prevent and relieve rheumatism and arthritis, a custom that began in the Middle Ages. Hindus often wear earrings of copper to prevent sciatica and ear infections.

But healing is not the metal's only perceived power. Copper set with jade was once considered the finest token of love for a young man to give to his beloved. In some Chinese dialects the word for copper (tong) sounds like the word "together." Copper bowls and shoes were once placed in the beds of bridal couples in northern China, symbolizing the hope that the couple would grow old together.

As for the frog on the Healing Meditation Candle (next page), many Native American tribes associated this water-loving creature with cleansing, hence with healing.

*Designer:* DIANA LIGHT

# HEALING MEDITATION CANDLE

**M**ODERN MEDICAL PRACTI-TIONERS RECOGNIZE THAT MEDITATION, OR SIMPLY CALMING THE SPIRIT AND MIND, CAN BE A BOON TO HEALING THE BODY AS WELL. WATCHING THE FLAME OF A CANDLE WHILE LETTING GO OF THOUGHTS AND STRESSES IS A SIM-PLE WAY TO ACHIEVE A PEACEFUL STATE OF MIND. THIS CANDLE IS WRAPPED IN COPPER WIRE AND DEC-ORATED WITH STONES AND A FROG FETISH, ALL CHOSEN FOR THEIR SYMBOLIC LINKS TO HEALING.

## THIS LITTLE LIGHT OF MINE, I'M GONNA LET IT SHINE.

Traditional gospel song

## MATERIALS

Pillar candle with 3 wicks

Fine copper mesh

5 loops of silver memory wire necklace

3 gold-colored changeable bead bars

Carved stone frog bead

Stone chip beads of blue agate, purple amethyst, green aventurine, hematite. red jasper, rose quartz

## TOOLS

Ruler

Craft knife

## INSTRUCTIONS

### 1.

Measure the height of the candle. Wrap copper mesh around the candle to find its circumference, and add $1/4$ inch (6 mm) for overlap. Cut the copper mesh to these measurements, then wrap around the candle.

### 2.

Wrap the memory wire necklace around the candle, arranging it to hold the copper mesh in place.

### 3.

Stack the stone chips and frog bead onto the bead bars, and thread them onto the memory wire necklace.

BAUMAN
NORMAL MODEL
FORD INC.
N.Y.

COLLAPS-A-FORM
S

MODEL 1963

*Designer:* LISA SARASOHN

# HONOR YOUR BELLY BELT

THE BELLY BELT CELEBRATES YOUR BODY'S MID-SECTION AS THE CENTER OF YOUR GREATER BEING, THE SOURCE OF THE LIFE ENERGY THAT ANIMATES YOUR CREATIVE POWER, DEEP WISDOM, AND CONNECTION. IN KOREAN, THE WORD FOR BELLY CENTER IS *TAN JEON*, OR ENERGY GARDEN. THE BELLY BELT, WITH ITS INNER POCKET, ALLOWS YOU TO ADORN YOUR BELLY'S CENTER WITH SYMBOLS OF POWER AND CREATIVITY, BOTH VISIBLE AND NOT.

## MATERIALS

$5/8$ yard (51.5 cm) of cotton fabric

Pattern pieces for center, sides, and pocket (see figure 1 page 89)

Paper

Thin cardboard

Fabric paints

Thread

2 D-rings, 1 inch (2.5 cm) diameter

## TOOLS

Steam iron

Tape measure

Scissors

Straight pins

Washable fabric-marking pen

Paintbrushes

Needle or sewing machine

## THE SPIRIT TENDS TOWARD PURITY BUT THE MIND DISTURBS IT.

*Tao te Ching*

# INSTRUCTIONS

### 1.

Wash and iron the fabric.

### 2.

To custom fit the pattern on page 89 to you, measure the circumference of your body 2 inches (5 cm) below your navel. The center piece of the pattern extends 20 inches (51 cm) across the front. Subtract this 20 inches (51 cm) from the circumference measurement. Divide the remainder in half to determine the base measurement for the side pieces. The right side piece will be this base measurement plus $1/2$ inch (1.3 cm) for a seam allowance and $1 1/4$ inches (3 cm) for fabric to enclose the D-rings. The left side piece will be the base measurement plus $1/2$ inch (1.3 cm) for seam allowances and 6 inches (15 cm) to pull through and past the D-rings.

### 3.

Enlarge the pattern pieces on page 89 to scale. Copy and cut out the pattern pieces for the pocket, center, and side pieces. Using additional sheets of paper, extend the length of each side piece at its narrower end according to your calculation in step 2.

### 4.

Fold the fabric along its width, and pin the pattern pieces to the fabric. Cut out one pocket, two center pieces (front and back), and two sets of side pieces (front and back for right and left sides.)

### 5.

Using the fabric-marking pen, mark the vertical center line on the right side of both the front and back center pieces.

### 6.

On paper, design the symbol you wish to wear over your belly's center to depict the spiritual wisdom and power of this energetic source-point. Use the fabric-marking pen to mark your design on the right side of the front center piece. If necessary, cut out circles and other shapes from thin cardboard to use as stencils and guides.

### 7.

Use fabric paints to realize your design, applying as many coats as needed. Let the paint dry completely.

### 8.

Prepare the pocket by folding over the top edge twice toward the wrong side of the fabric to make a finished $1/4$-inch (6 mm) hem. Press and stitch. Repeat at the bottom edge. Fold the top toward the wrong side of the fabric to make the top flap; press. Fold the bottom toward the wrong side of the fabric to make the pocket's lower edge; press. Fold the pocket's side edges toward the wrong side of the fabric; press. Mark the pocket's vertical center line.

### 9.

Matching the vertical lines, center the pocket on the right side of the back center piece, and pin. Starting at the top of one side edge, stitch down one side, across the bottom, and up the other side, reinforcing the top of the side seams with extra stitching.

### 10.

Seam allowances are $1/4$ inch (6 mm). With right sides together, stitch right and left side pieces to the back center piece. Stitch right and left side pieces to the front center piece.

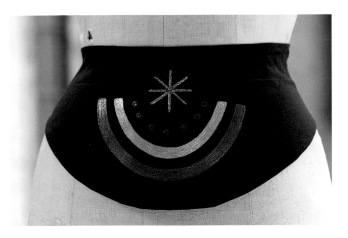

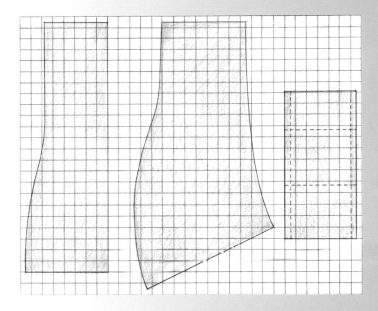

*Figure 1*

### 11.

With right sides together, pin the front to the back. Stitch, leaving an opening at the bottom edge of the center piece for turning right side out. Clip curves, and turn right side out. Turn in the seam allowance and slip stitch the opening closed.

### 12

Slip the end of the right side piece through the two D-rings, folding the end of the side piece onto the back of the belt so that the edge rests 1¼ inches (3 cm) below the straight edges of the D-rings. Stitch along the edge to secure. Press lightly, ironing on the back of the belt and avoiding the design area.

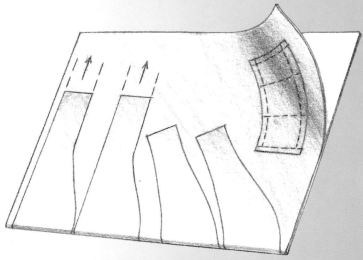

*Figure 2*

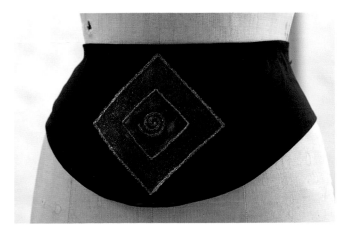

# *About The* BELLY

**D**esigner Lisa Sarasohn notes: "In Japanese, the belly is termed hara, meaning home of the soul. In Chinese, the belly center is known to be 'the Gate of the Mysterious Female.' In English, we use the word 'gutsy' to describe a woman who is spirited, brave, sensuous. The belly center is the source-point of our physical and spiritual vitality.

"Cultures around the world have recognized the significance of the body's center throughout time, cultivating the life force centered there with belly-energizing traditions of dance, healing arts, and spiritual practice."

Yet in contemporary times, people, particularly women, have been taught to be ashamed of their bellies. To worry when they are too large, to tuck them in at all times, to flatten and compress them if you want to be thought attractive.

The Honor Your Belly Belt is just one part of a program Lisa has created to reclaim this sacred center of the body. Using dance, art, writing, and more, she leads workshops and classes in Asheville, North Carolina, to encourage class participants to become more aware of the belly's power. And she has exercises and provocative belly thoughts on her Web site at www.honoryourbelly.com.

She says, "The vital energy stored in, and radiating from, your body's center is pro-creative power in the largest sense. It is the power to promote creation akin to the Power of Being which infuses the universe. Adorning your belly with sacred symbols acknowledges the spiritual power you carry within you."

*Designer:* FRANÇOISE HESSELINK

# RECEPTIVITY SALTS

A NICE WARM BATH IS THE CURE FOR PLENTY OF SMALL BODILY ILLS FROM ACHES OF THE BONES TO ACHES OF THE HEART. THESE CUSTOM-BLENDED BATH SALTS CONTAIN ESSENTIAL OILS THAT NOT ONLY RELAX THE BODY, BUT ARE BELIEVED TO AID IN OPENING THE MIND AND SPIRIT FOR MEDITATION OR DREAM-FILLED SLEEP.

THE SOUL SHOULD ALWAYS STAND AJAR, READY TO WELCOME THE ECSTATIC EXPERIENCE.

*Emily Dickinson*
American poet

DESIGNER NOTE:

*Use good-quality essential oils since quality can vary greatly. Keep the salt away from moisture. If damp, it will clump. Use a chopstick to stir and loosen it.*

CAUTION: *These salts should NOT be used during pregnancy.*

## MATERIALS

1/2 cup plus 2 tbsp. (140 gr) plain coarse bath salt or coarse sea salt

1/2 cup plus 2 tbsp. (140 gr) Epsom salts

1/4 cup plus 2 tsp (65 gr) baking soda

10 drops mugwort essential oil

25 drops lemon essential oil

15 drops elemi essential oil

20 drops lavender essential oil

Bottle with cork large enough to hold 12 ounces (360 mL)

## TOOLS

Food processor

Plastic funnel

## INSTRUCTIONS

1.

Grind the coarse salt in the food processor until almost smooth.

2.

Add the Epsom salts and baking soda, and mix.

3.

Add the oils and mix again.

4.

Pour with the funnel into the clean, dry bottle. Do not pack tightly.

# LOVE WAS BEFORE THE LIGHT BEGAN; WHEN LIGHT IS OVER, LOVE SHALL BE.

*The Thousand and One Nights*

# *Receptivity*
# SALTS RITUAL
## BY FRANCOISE HESSELINK

To begin, make sure your bathroom and tub are clean and uncluttered. Choose objects you want around you, such as statues, images, crystals, stones, candles, or music, and place them in the bathroom.

To clear the energy in the room, you can use the Smudge Pot Ritual (page 40), or light a candle or incense. You can play music, if you wish, or you can pray.

Fill the tub with warm water. When full, add one to three spoonfuls of the bath salts. Stir well.

State your intention, aloud if possible. For example, to remember your dreams, to do lucid dreaming, to obtain guidance for a specific question, or simply to open up to a meditative state.

Stir the water again, step in, and enjoy!

*Designer:* JANE DAVIS

# BEADED VIAL

Essential oils, flower essences, and aromatherapy essences have become part of the apothecary for contemporary well-being. This small beaded vial is perfect for carrying such precious liquids, or for keeping a cache of sacred water, healing dirt, or bright crystals. It can be tucked into a pocket, worn like jewelry, or displayed on an altar. Choose beads that have colors or significance relating to the contents.

ANOINT AND CHEER OUR SOILED FACE
WITH THE ABUNDANCE OF THY GRACE;
KEEP FAR OUR FOES; GIVE PEACE
AT HOME; WHERE THOU ART GUIDE,
NO ILL CAN COME.

*Ninth-century psalm*

## MATERIALS

Small glass vial with an indented rim

24 inches (61 cm) of cotton or leather cord,
  1/16 inch (1.5mm) wide

12 size 3.3 mm cylinder beads

8 size 6 seed beads

4 size 6 hexagon beads

Note: all the above beads must have holes large enough
  to fit onto the cord

Size B beading thread

24 size 11 seed beads in main color

4 size 8 seed beads for large center dangle

1 size 6 triangle bead for large center dangle

1 drop bead for large center dangle

1 small oval bead for small center dangle

3 size 11 seed beads in bronze color for small
  center dangle

Accent bead for top of cork

1 large bead or crystal to string onto the cord at the top
  of the piece, with a hole large enough to fit two
  widths of the cord (optional)

## TOOLS

Scissors

Glue

Craft knife or small straight pin

Size 11 beading needle

NOTE: The following instructions are for the vial shown. You may need to adjust the number of beads in the dangles for different-sized vials.

## INSTRUCTIONS

### 1.

Tie one end of the cord around the rim of the vial, leaving a 2-inch (5 cm) tail. String three cylinder beads, one size 6 bead, one hexagon bead, and one size 6 bead onto the short tail of the cord. Tie a knot next to the last bead strung, and cut the cord next to the knot.

Repeat step 1 with the other end of the cord, adjusting the length of the cord to the desired finished length before tying the first knot.

### 2.

Thread the needle with a 24-inch (61 cm) length of thread. Pass the needle around or through the cord next to one of the knots on the vial rim, and tie the two thread ends into a knot, leaving a 6-inch (15 cm) tail to weave in later.

### 3.

For the large dangle, string one hexagon bead, one size 6 bead, one cylinder bead,* one size 8 bead, 7 size 11 beads in main color, one size 8 bead, one cylinder bead*, one size 6 bead, the triangle bead, one size 6 bead, three size 11 beads in main color, one drop bead, and three size 11 seed beads in main color. Skip the last 7 beads strung and pass through the size 6 bead, the triangle bead, and the next size 6 bead. String a mirror image of the first side of the dangle (the beads listed between the asterisks in reverse order); see figure 1. Pass the needle around or through the cord next to the knot on the opposite side of the vial.

*Figure 1*

**4.**

For the small inner dangle, pass the needle back through the hexagon bead and the size 6 bead. String one cylinder bead, two size 11 seed beads in the main color, one small oval bead, and three size 11 bronze seed beads. Pass the needle back through the small oval bead, and then string two size 11 seed beads in the main color and one cylinder bead. Pass the needle through the size 6 bead and the hexagon bead on the opposite side of the vial and around or through the cord. Tie a knot and hide the thread in the strands of beads for about 1 inch (2.5 cm), then cut close to the beads. Hide the 6-inch (15 cm) tail in the same manner.

**5.**

To decorate the cork, either glue a bead to the top of the cork (hollowing out the center slightly if needed, with the craft knife), or string beads on a small straight pin and press the pin into the top of the cork.

*Optional: Fold the top of the neck cord in half and string a large crystal onto the cord, then slide it down near the top of the vial.*

ABANDON THE SEARCH FOR GOD. LOOK FOR HIM BY TAKING YOURSELF AS THE STARTING POINT. LEARN WHO IT IS WITHIN YOU WHO MAKES EVERYTHING HIS OWN AND SAYS, "MY GOD, MY MIND, MY THOUGHT, MY SOUL, MY BODY." LEARN THE SOURCE OF SORROW, JOY, LOVE, HATE. IF YOU CAREFULLY INVESTIGATE THESE MATTERS, YOU WILL FIND GOD IN YOUR SELF.

Gnostic teacher

# Rituals Of The Ages

"God never occurs to you in person but always in action," Mahatma Gandhi said. Throughout time and across all cultures, seekers have created rituals to open their own hearts, or invoke the presence of a spirit or spirits greater than themselves. Such rituals may be as simple as placing a single beautiful blossom in a chipped vase and contemplating it with an awareness of the Japanese concept of *wabi-sabi*, seeing the beauty in imperfection. Or the rituals may be as rich with imagery and activity as the celebration of the Day of the Dead in Mexico. In all cases it is the intention of the participants that brings meaning to the ritual more than any specific action or thing.

In this section you will find a diverse offering of projects drawn from the rituals of various belief systems. You may wish to discover more about the specific faith behind each ritual, or you may use the information and instructions here to fashion a ritual that is distinctly your own.

JON BOWER

THE LEAST OF THINGS WITH A MEANING IS WORTH MORE IN LIFE THAN THE GREATEST OF THINGS WITHOUT IT.

*Carl Jung*
Swiss psychiatrist

Designer: ANNE ASHLEY

# TIBETAN PRAYER FLAG

T HE PRAYER FLAGS OF TIBET HAVE PRAYERS FOR PEACE, LOVE, AND COMPASSION WRITTEN ON THEM. THEY ARE DECORATED WITH THE IMAGE OF A POWERFUL HORSE THAT CARRIES THESE PRAYERS THROUGHOUT THE WORLD. COLORED RED, BLUE, GREEN, WHITE, AND YELLOW, THE FLAGS REPRESENT THE FOUR ELEMENTS AND THE EARTH. MADE OF LIGHT MATERIAL OR PAPER, THE FLAGS ARE HUNG OUTSIDE SUBJECT TO THE ELEMENTS AND ARE MEANT TO DISINTEGRATE OVER TIME AND BE REPLACED WITH NEW FLAGS AND NEW PRAYERS. USE THE HORSE STENCIL TO DECORATE YOUR FLAG AND WRITE PRAYERS IN YOUR OWN WORDS.

WHAT IS LIFE? IT IS THE FLASH OF A FIREFLY IN THE NIGHT. IT IS THE BREATH OF A BUFFALO IN THE WINTERTIME. IT IS THE LITTLE SHADOW WHICH RUNS ACROSS THE GRASS AND LOSES ITSELF IN THE SUNSET.

*Crowfoot*

Native American warrior and orator

## MATERIALS

Wind Horse stencil (below) enlarged to twice its size

Heavy cardboard

2 pieces each of cloth that measure $13^{1}/2$ x 11 inches (34.5 x 28 cm) in red, blue, green, yellow and white

11 strips each of cloth that measures 1 x 10 inches (2.5 x 25.5 cm) in red, blue, green, yellow and white

Black paint

Rope long enough to hang the flags between trees or posts you have chosen

Red thread

## TOOLS

Scissors

Craft knife

Stencil brush

Pins

Sewing machine or hand-sewing needle

## INSTRUCTIONS

### 1.

Photocopy the enlarged Wind Horse stencil and trace it onto the heavy cardboard. Use the craft knife to cut away the interior of the stencil.

### 2.

Center the stencil on one of the larger pieces of cloth, and use the stencil brush to apply black paint inside the stencil openings to create the Wind Horse image. Make sure to dab paint over the edges of the stencil or the image will smear. Carefully remove the stencil, and allow flag to dry. Repeat for remaining pieces of cloth.

### 3.

Attach the flags to the rope by folding the top edge over the rope and pinning it to the other side of the fabric. (You can arrange the colors in any order you prefer.) In between the flags, pin one strip of each color. Repeat until all five colors of flags have been pinned to the rope. Repeat the color order of the first five flags and strips with the remaining materials.

### 4.

Sew the flags and strips across the top edge using the red thread. Remove the pins.

### 5.

Taper the bottoms of the strips as shown in the project, so that the shortest strip measures 4 inches (10 cm) below the rope, and the longest measures 9 inches (23 cm).

### 6.

Write your hopes, wishes, and dreams on the strips, and hang the rope, allowing the Wind Horse to carry them off to be fulfilled.

*Designer:* TERRY TAYLOR

# TORAN

THE TORAN IS A CLOTH OR PAPER BANNER PAINTED, BEADED, OR EMBROIDERED WITH SYMBOLIC IMAGES OF GOOD FORTUNE AND HUNG OVER THE ENTRANCE OF INDIAN HOMES TO WELCOME VISITORS AND ATTRACT GOOD LUCK AND PROSPERITY. THE PAISLEY DESIGN INCORPORATES THE *BOTEH* MOTIF, WHICH IS BELIEVED TO HAVE EVOLVED FROM REPRESENTATIONS OF THE TREE OF LIFE. IT IS OFTEN LIKENED TO THE MANGO, WHICH IS A SYMBOL OF GOOD FORTUNE AND GENEROSITY.

THE TRUE MYSTIC IS NOT A RECLUSIVE SAINT WHO AVOIDS OTHERS. THE TRUE MYSTIC LIVES ALONGSIDE OTHER PEOPLE—COMING AND GOING, EATING AND SLEEPING, BUYING AND SELLING, MARRYING AND CHATTING—BUT NOT FOR A MOMENT DOES HE FORGET GOD.

*Abu Sa'id Ibn Abi L Khayr*
Sufi sage

DESIGNER NOTE:

*If you wish to use this toran outdoors, laminate it to protect it from the elements. You can do it yourself, or take it to your local copy shop.*

# MATERIALS

Template below

Wrapping paper

Colored tissue papers

Aerosol glue or glue stick

# TOOLS

Pencil

Ruler

Scissors

Stapler

Decorative-edge scissors

Decorative hole punches

# INSTRUCTIONS

### 1.

Photocopy the template (enlarge the pattern as desired).

### 2.

Measure the doorway you wish to adorn and cut a length of wrapping paper slightly longer than the doorway's length. Make sure the height of the wrapping paper equals that of the template.

### 3.

Fanfold the length of wrapping paper with a width that fits the template.

### 4.

Staple the template to the folded paper. Cut out the shape with plain or decorative scissors as desired.

### 5.

To create the smaller designs on the toran, fanfold one color of tissue paper for each shape. Draw a shape on the fold that you wish to use: a paisley, oval, rectangle, or any shape desired.

### 6.

Use the decorative punches to make designs on the shapes while they are folded. Then, cut out the shapes with decorative-edge scissors.

### 7.

Adhere the shapes to the background paper with aerosol glue or a glue stick.

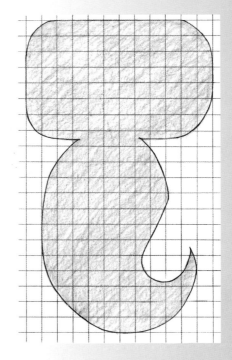

*Designer:* JUDI ASHE

# PURGE POT

WHEN IT IS TIME TO SHED THE UNNECESSARY EMOTIONAL BAGGAGE THAT HAS BEEN WEIGHING YOU DOWN, THE PURGE POT CAN BE YOUR TOOL. THE PURGE POT RITUAL ON PAGE 108 WILL TELL YOU HOW. INSTRUCTIONS FOR MAKING THE PURGE POT ARE ON PAGE 36; INSTRUCTIONS FOR MAKING THE LOW-FIRE KILN ARE ON PAGE 37.

HOLDING ON TO ANGER IS LIKE GRASPING A HOT COAL WITH THE INTENT OF THROWING IT AT SOMEONE ELSE; YOU ARE THE ONE GETTING BURNED.

*Siddhartha Gautama Buddha*
Founder of Buddhism

# *The Purge Pot*
# RITUAL
## BY JUDI ASHE

The Purge Pot is a tool for releasing. This ritual is based on an ancient tradition called "The Burning Bowl," used by many indigenous cultures throughout time. It uses the element of fire to help us release things that we may not need anymore in our lives, therefore making room within ourselves for growth and new manifestations. This ritual is a potent experience whether it is done in a group or alone. It is nice to work with the Purge Pot often, especially when one is going through a major life transition, or dealing with a lot of decisions. Here is the general idea of a Purge Pot ritual:

The Purge Pot is made in two parts. The base is an urn or a vessel to collect the ashes. The lid is made to hold a tea candle in it. Remove the lid and place it next to the urn. Light the candle. Take a moment to get centered and quiet within. When you feel ready, begin to reflect upon those aspects of your life that you feel ready to release. Have paper and pencil handy. Write down these aspects on the paper, being sure to begin by writing, "I release into the fire..."

When you are ready, focus yourself totally on the aspect you are releasing as you fold up the paper and light it with the tea candle flame. Drop your burning paper into the urn and see it vaporizing before you, turning into ashes, transformed and released forever. You may find that more and more things come up that you would like to release, and that you end up burning many pieces of paper before you are done. This is a great ritual for gaining clarity about oneself. When you are finished burning the paper, let the ashes cool. Then, as a final part of this ceremony, take the urn with the ashes in it and dispose of them in whatever manner you feel fit, i.e., bury them outside or scatter them in a river. When you release the ashes from the urn, it is recommended that a prayer of gratitude be given for these things that were a part of you, and simply let them go with love.

SKIP WADE

IN THE BEGINNING NOTHING COMES.
IN THE MIDDLE NOTHING STAYS.
IN THE END NOTHING GOES.

*Milarepa*
Tibetan yogi

*Designer:* DIANA LIGHT

# BOTTLE TREE

AN OLD TRADITION IN THE SOUTHERN UNITED STATES, THE BOTTLE TREE ACTUALLY HAS ITS ROOTS IN THE CONGO. CLASSICALLY MADE WITH A CEDAR TREE STRIPPED OF ITS FRONDS, THE BRANCHES ARE THEN HUNG WITH BRIGHT COLORED BOTTLES TO ATTRACT EVIL SPIRITS. THESE SPIRITS ARE TRAPPED IN THE BOTTLES UNTIL A WIND COMES TO BLOW THEM SAFELY AWAY FROM YOUR HOME. OUR CONTEMPORARY VERSION USES PRE-CUT LUMBER AND INCORPORATES A CONGO MOTIF IN ITS DESIGN. IT CAN BE USED OUTSIDE OR ON AN INNER THRESHOLD. COBALT BLUE IS THE PREFERRED BOTTLE COLOR, BUT YOU MAY USE ANY COLORS.

SOMETIMES I THINK WE'RE ALONE IN THE UNIVERSE, AND SOMETIMES I THINK WE'RE NOT. IN EITHER CASE, THE IDEA IS QUITE STAGGERING.

*Arthur C. Clarke*
British writer

## MATERIALS

Wooden fence post, 4 feet (1.2 m) tall

3/4-inch-thick (2 cm) plywood, 22 inches (56 cm) square

4 galvanized screws, 2 inches (5 cm) long

Fence post ball top

12 dowels, 1/2 inch (1.5 cm) in diameter, 12 inches (30.5 cm) long

Brown and black acrylic craft paint

Clear spray enamel

12 blue glass bottles

## TOOLS

Safety glasses

Pencil

Straightedge at least 36 inches (91.5 cm) long

Power drill

Bit for pre-drilling screw holes

Screwdriver

1/2-inch (1.5 cm) wood-boring bit

Assorted paintbrushes

Wood glue

Rinse cup and paper towels

## INSTRUCTIONS

### 1.

Determine the center of the plywood square. Wearing eye protection, use one screw to attach the fence post to the square from beneath, putting the screw straight into the center of the square and the post. Use the other three screws to anchor by screwing them in at an angle for added strength.

### 2.

Screw the ball top to the top of the post.

### 3.

Mark the placement of the dowels on the post, evenly spacing four vertical rows with three dowels each, staggered so that the opposite sides are the same.

### 4.

Use the wood-boring bit to drill holes for the dowels, working at an angle from above.

### 5.

Paint the entire piece, including the dowels, brown. Allow to dry.

### 6.

With the project photo as a guide, use the straightedge to draw graphics. Paint the graphics black and allow to dry. Insert the dowels, tipped with wood glue, into the post. Allow to dry.

### 7.

Spray the entire piece with clear enamel. Allow to dry.

### 8.

Hang the blue bottles on the dowels.

*Designer:* DIANA LIGHT

# CELTIC EMBROIDERED TAROT POUCH

THE TAROT IS USED BY SOME FOR DIVINATION, BUT MANY HAVE FOUND THAT THE ARCHETYPES REPRESENTED IN THE DECK CAN BE WINDOWS TO THE SUB-CONSCIOUS. NO MATTER HOW YOU USE IT, A TAROT DECK IS WORTHY OF A BEAUTI-FUL CONTAINER FOR STORING AND TRANSPORTING IT. THIS SIMPLE BAG CAN BE MADE OF VELVET, SILK, OR TAPESTRY FABRIC AND EMBROIDERED WITH A SYMBOL THAT HAS MEANING FOR THE MAKER. THE CELTIC DOUBLE SPIRAL SHOWN HERE IS MEANT, LIKE THE *YIN YANG* SYMBOL, TO REPRESENT THE DUALITY OF EXISTENCE AND THE BAL-ANCE THAT MUST BE MAINTAINED BETWEEN OPPOSITES FOR A FULL LIFE.

THE WORD OF GOD MUST ALWAYS BE HEARD QUITE SPECIFICALLY AND IN A NEW WAY, VARYING ACCORDING TO THE CONDITIONS UNDER WHICH IT IS PREACHED. FAITH IS NOT AN ACCEPTANCE OF GENERAL, ABSTRACT TRUTHS, BUT AN ANSWER AND A DECISION AT A CERTAIN TIME AND IN A VERY CERTAIN PLACE.

*J. L. Hromadka*
Czechoslovakian theologian

## MATERIALS

7 x 22-inch (18 x 56 cm) piece of purple velvet

White gel pen

Adhesive-backed tearaway fabric backing, larger than
  template (see step 2)

Gold metallic embroidery floss

2 lengths of gold cording, each 15 inches (38 cm) long

Purple thread

## TOOLS

Craft knife

Embroidery needle

Tape

Scissors

Ethyl cyanoacrylate glue or other product to stop fraying

Straight pins

Sewing machine

Safety pin

## INSTRUCTIONS

### 1.

With right sides out, fold the velvet along its width to
form a 7 x 11-inch (18 x 28cm) rectangle.

### 2.

Create a template of the design using the embroidered
image in photo.

### 3.

Center the template pieces on the velvet; trace around
them with the white gel pen.

### 4.

Affix the tearaway fabric to the back of the velvet on
which you've traced the design. This will stabilize the
velvet as you embroider.

### 5.

Separate the floss into three-strand sections and chain
stitch along the design's lines (see figure 1). To chain
stitch, bring the needle up from the bottom, then back
down through the same hole. Pull the thread through,
leaving a small loop. Bring the needle up a stitch in front
of the loop, and then through it. Pull tightly, repeat.

### 6.

Cover the chain stitch with satin stitch, so that it's completely hidden (see figure 2). To satin stitch along the
stitch line, bring the threaded needle up right next to the
edge of the chain stitch at one end; then insert the needle
directly across on the other side of the chain, covering the
chain stitch with the line of thread. For the next stitch,
bring the needle up directly below the first satin stitch,
and insert directly below the second on the other side.

Continue working down the chain stitch until it is covered. On the triangle part, satin stitch from each point towards the center, bringing the needle up on the outside of one side of the figure and inserting it on the outside of the opposite side. Your stitches will grow increasingly wider as you work the design. Tear away fabric backing.

### 7.

Wrap tape around the edges of the cord to prevent fraying. Secure the ends with gold floss, then remove the tape. Apply glue to stop fraying.

On the back of the fabric, mark lines $^{1}/_{2}$ inch (1.5 cm) from the long sides.

### 8.

To make the tube through which you'll thread the cord, place the velvet wrong side up on your work surface. Working on an edge that's 7 inches (18 cm) long, fold the velvet up $^{1}/_{4}$ inch (6 mm) as if you were making a hem; at the same time, fold the sides perpendicular to your fold (which are the side seam allowances of the pouch) up $^{1}/_{2}$ inch (1.5 cm). Then fold the velvet 1 inch (2.5 cm). Pin in place and sew. Repeat on other end.

### 9.

Fold the velvet right side in, pin in place, and sew on the marked lines (from step 8), from the folded corners to 1 inch (2.5 cm) away from the tube hem.

### 10.

Turn the pouch right side out, and place it on your work surface so that the opening is facing away from you. Run the safety pin through one end of a cord. Coming from the left, thread the cord through a tube by pushing the safety pin forward from the exterior with your fingers.

Repeat with the other tube. Both ends will come out on the right side of the bag. Knot them. Repeat the process with the other cord, threading it from the right side so that both ends come out on the right. Knot them.

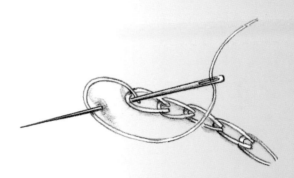

*Figure 1*

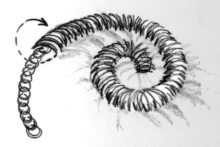

*Figure 2*

*Designer:* JANE DAVIS

# AMULET BAG

**M**ANY SPIRITUAL TRADITIONS ENCOURAGE WEARING A SACRED OBJECT AROUND THE NECK TO PROTECT THE SPIRIT, BRING GOOD FORTUNE, AND/OR MAKE US MINDFUL OF SOME ASPECT OF OUR BELIEFS. LEATHER FROM AN ANIMAL, STONES AND CLAY FROM THE EARTH, AND MOLTEN GLASS—A SYMBOL OF TRANSFORMATION— COME TOGETHER TO MAKE THIS POUCH AS MEANINGFUL AS THE OBJECT WITHIN.

YOU CAN SOMETIMES COUNT EVERY ORANGE ON A TREE BUT NEVER ALL THE TREES IN A SINGLE ORANGE.

*A. K. Ramanujan*
Indian poet

## MATERIALS

Scrap of suede $2^1/2$ x 3 inches (6.5 x 7.5 cm)

24 inches (61 cm) of leather or cotton cord thin enough to string all the beads

7 grams of size 6 seed beads

3 clay or raku beads, $3/8$ to $1/2$ inch (9.5 mm to 1.5 cm) in diameter

Amethyst crystal, approx. $1/4$ x $1^1/4$ inches (6 mm x 3 cm)

## TOOLS

Leather glue, or cement that is flexible when dry

Scissors

Hole punch (optional)

## INSTRUCTIONS

### 1.

Fold the scrap of suede along its length, overlapping the edges about $1/8$ inch (3 mm), and carefully glue them together so you have a tube about $1 1/2$ x $2 1/2$ inches (4 cm x 6.5 cm). Allow to dry (see figure 1).

### 2.

Flatten the tube so that the glued seam is in the center back. Cut the bottom of the flattened tube (cutting through both the front and back layers as one), beginning at the fold about $3/4$ inch (2 cm) from the bottom, tapering down to a point at the center, then back up to the other side. Carefully glue the front and back together along the bottom edge. Let dry (see figures 2 and 3).

### 3.

Cut the top edge in the same manner as the bottom, except make the center rounded, rather than a point. Fold the back to the back and the front to the front of the bag.

### 4.

Cut a small hole with the hole punch or scissors at the bottom point of the bag, about $1/8$ inch (3 mm) from the edge. Cut two holes at each side of the bag, one $1/8$ inch (3 mm) from the top and the other $1/4$ inch (6 mm) further down the side.

### 5.

Tie a knot $1/2$ inch (1.5 cm) from one end of the cord, and string three size 6 beads and one clay or raku bead. Pass the cord through the hole at the bottom of the bag and back through the large bead. String three more size 6 beads. Pull the cord so the beads are held snugly in place.

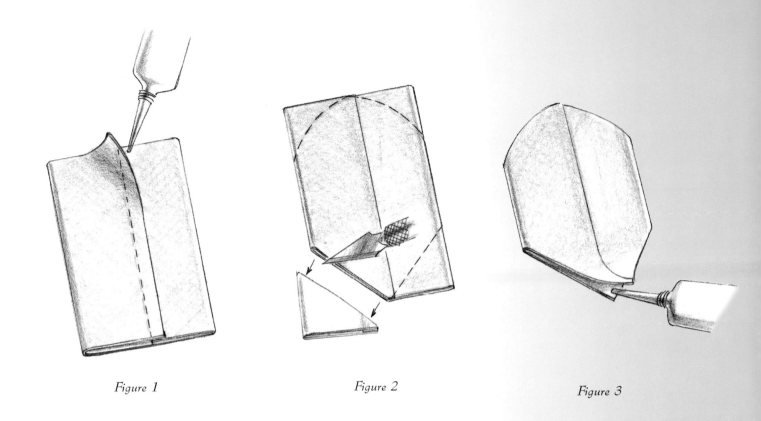

*Figure 1*  *Figure 2*  *Figure 3*

Tie a knot next to the last bead strung, and cut the cord about $1/2$ inch (1.5 cm) from the knot.

### 6.

Tie a knot $1/2$ inch (1.5 cm) from one end of the remaining cord, and string one size 6 bead, one clay or raku bead, and three size 6 beads. Pass the cord through the two holes on one side of the bag, beginning by going in the bottom hole and out the top hole. Then pass the cord through the two holes on the other side of the bag, by going in the top hole and out the bottom hole. String three of the size 6 beads, one of the clay or raku beads, and one of the size 6 beads. Adjust the cord so that it is the length you want, then tie a knot next to the last bead strung. Cut the cord about $1/2$ inch (1.5 cm) from the knot.

### 7.

Cut a small horizontal slit in the center front flap, smaller than the diameter of the amethyst crystal, and a little more than $1/8$ inch (3 mm) from the edge. Be careful not to make the hole too big or the crystal will fall through. Squeeze the crystal into place so that it hangs snugly in the hole in the flap in front of the bag.

# Dream Work

Most of us spend a third of our lives asleep. During a typical night of sleep, we dream some three to five times for periods of 10 to 30 minutes each time. Science has offered numerous theories to explain how we dream, but for spiritual seekers, the "how" of dreaming is less important than the "what" and "why."

Psychoanalyst Carl Jung took both a scientific and a mystical perspective on dreams. Like Sigmund Freud, he saw dreams as a tool in analysis, the voice of the unconscious; but he also believed they were part of a larger collective unconscious, or spiritual plane. He wrote: "In each of us there is another whom we do not know. He speaks to us in dreams and tells us how differently he sees us from the way we see ourselves. When, therefore, we find ourselves in a difficult situation to which there is no solution, he can sometimes kindle a light that radically alters our attitude—the very attitude that led to the difficult situation."

Jung was only one in a long line of teachers who believed that dreams have a greater power. Aboriginal Australians, Native American visionaries, Hindu mystics, Christian saints, ancient Egyptians, and contemporary seers have all used dreams in various ways to pursue spiritual work. Aesculapius, Roman god of healing, was believed to do his work during the dreams of the sick. Ancient Greek believers slept in special rooms in certain temples so they could receive divine guidance in their dreams. Black Elk said that, among the Sioux, an individual's dreams might be acted out by different members of the tribe because they were deemed to be important messages to the community.

The process of recording and recalling dreams on a regular basis is a common tool recognized and used in contemporary psychotherapy. As we become more adept at recalling our dreams, we may desire to do things prior to sleeping in order to invite them in. The projects in this section are designed to enhance such dream work.

JON BOWER

# SOMETIMES DREAMS ARE WISER THAN WAKING.

## *Black Elk*

Oglala Sioux holy man and seer

*Designer:* GABE CYR

# DREAM DOLL

O NE OF THESE SOFT, NIGHTTIME COMPANIONS CAN SIT ON YOUR BED OR A TABLE NEXT TO IT TO GENTLY REMIND YOU TO DANCE IN YOUR DREAMS. THE MESSAGE YOUR DREAM DOLL CARRIES CAN BE ONE THAT IS TIMELESS, OR SOMETHING YOU CHANGE TO FIT THE WORK YOU WANT TO DO IN YOUR DREAMS.

## MEDITATE AND REALIZE THAT THIS WORLD IS FULL OF THE PRESENCE OF GOD.

*The Upanishads*

Figures 1-5: 1 square = $1/2$ inch

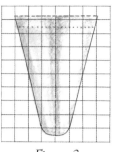

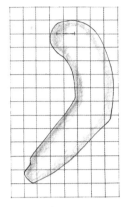

*Figure 3*

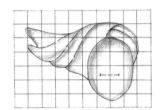

*Figure 4*

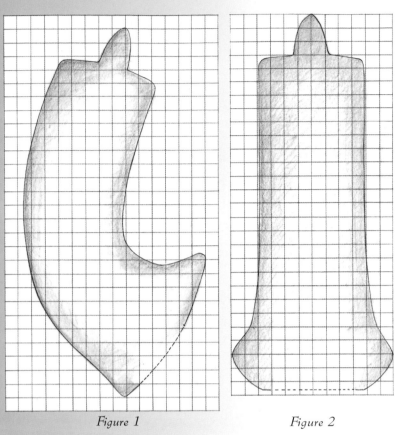

*Figure 5*

*Figure 1*

*Figure 2*

## MATERIALS

Doll pattern pieces (figure 1 or 2),
  enlarged to scale

Stiff paper (large enough to transfer pattern onto)

$1/4$ yard (23 cm) each of two differently patterned
  fabrics

Gel pen, in color to complement fabric

Thread, in color that matches fabric

Stuffing material

Fusible web (optional)

Fabric scraps or wide ribbon

White and flesh-toned acrylic paint

Matte medium (optional)

Colored pencils in brown, white, and rose

Black fine-line pen

Red gel pen

Embellishing materials such as beads, charms,
  buttons, etc.

## TOOLS

Scissors

Sewing machine or hand-sewing needle

Straight pins

Assorted paintbrushes

# INSTRUCTIONS

### 1.

Photocopy the pattern pieces on page 124, enlarged to scale. Use tracing paper to transfer them onto the stiff paper. Make 2 arm pieces. Cut them out. These are your templates.

### 2.

Fold each piece of fabric in half along its width with the wrong side of the fabric facing out. Place the body piece template on one fabric, and the two arms (figure 4), leg piece (figure 3), and head/hair piece (figure 5) on the other fabric. Trace the pattern pieces using the gel pen.

### 3.

Keeping the fabric folded, sew directly on the lines, leaving open where the template indicates. Cut out the pieces and clip all the inside curves. Turn out only the legs. Sew a line down the middle, as marked on the pattern, then stuff each of the two channels you've created. Stuff lightly near the open end.

### 4.

With the body piece still wrong side out, insert the leg piece, pointy end first, completely into the opening left at the bottom of the body, until the raw edges of the fabrics match. Sew the opening shut.

### 5.

In the center of only one layer of the body, make a vertical slit 1 1/2 inches (4 cm) long. Reach in and pull the legs out, turning the entire body right side out in the process.

### 6.

On the arms, slit only one layer as marked on the paper pattern. Turn right side out and stuff. Sew the slit closed, without distorting the upper arm, or attach a small piece of matching fabric over the slit using fusible web and an iron.

### 7.

Decide on the arm positions. They might both thrust up, or face out to the sides, or be in front of the body; or they might point in different directions. Even slight variations in placement create very different looks. Pin into place, then sew to the body.

### 8.

Determine which way you want the hair to blow. With the head still wrong side out, and the hair blowing in the direction you want, slit only the layer of fabric that is on top, as marked on the paper pattern. Make sure you've clipped the seam allowance, then turn right side out. As marked on the paper pattern, carefully mark the oval shape of the face, as well as the hair lines, on the side that hasn't been slit. Lightly stuff the hair area; it's no problem if the stuffing laps over into the face area. Sew the face oval, then the hair lines. Add more stuffing to the face oval.

### 9.

Fit the neck stub into the head slit on the body, and sew it in place.

### 10.

Illustrate the face using the paint, pens, and pencils. Decorate with beads, charms, buttons, etc. If you like, you can use cardboard, paper and/or fabric to create a banner to attach to the doll with an inspirational saying.

*Designer:* DIANA LIGHT

# DREAM DECANTER

TINTED GLASS IS BELIEVED TO IMPART THE ENERGY OF ITS COLOR TO THE LIQUID INSIDE. A BEDSIDE DECANTER FOR HOLDING DRINKING WATER CAN BE PAINTED IN THE COLOR YOU CHOOSE, PERHAPS TO INFLUENCE THE TENOR OF YOUR DREAMS. WE SELECTED BLUE BECAUSE IT IS THOUGHT TO HAVE A CALMING EFFECT, AND BECAUSE IT HAS BEEN TRADITIONALLY ASSOCIATED WITH THE SKY, HOLINESS. AND PURITY.

THE DEEPER BLUE BECOMES, THE MORE URGENTLY IT SUMMONS MAN TOWARDS THE INFINITE, THE MORE IT AROUSES IN HIM A LONGING FOR PURITY AND, ULTIMATELY, FOR THE SUPERSENSUAL.

*Wassily Kandinsky*
Russian abstract painter

## MATERIALS

Clear glass decanter

Masking tape

Green, blue, and purple transparent glass paints that are permanent and can be hand-washed

Glass paint diluent

Newspaper

Wax paper

## TOOLS

Craft knife

Cotton swabs

## INSTRUCTIONS

### 1.

Wash and dry the decanter.

### 2.

Use masking tape to cover the lip of the decanter $1/4$ inch deep.

### 3.

Fill each applicator bottle with one color of glass paint. Add diluent to each bottle to thin the glass paint to a consistency that will drip down the decanter.

### 4.

This project is very messy, so protect your workspace with the newspaper. Turn the decanter upside down onto a piece of wax paper. Squeeze blue glass paint around the base every $3/4$ inch (2 cm), using enough so that the paint drips down the decanter. (You may pour the blue paint that runs off the decanter and onto the wax paper back into the bottle.)

### 5.

Repeat the process with the green glass paint, dripping it between the blue glass paint.

Fill in any clear spaces with the purple glass paint. Let the paint dry to the touch.

### 6.

Remove the masking tape. Because glass paints are toxic, use the craft knife and cotton swabs moistened with water to remove any paint that may have seeped through from around the lip of the decanter. Allow to dry, following the manufacturer's instructions.

SKIP WADE

YEARS OF DIGGING THE EARTH
SEARCHING FOR THE BLUE SKY,
PILING UP LAYER UPON LAYER
OF MEDIOCRITY.
THEN ONE DARK NIGHT
THE CEILING BLEW OFF,
AND THE WHOLE STRUCTURE
DISAPPEARED INTO EMPTINESS.

*Muso*

Zen poet

*Dream Work*

*Designer:* DIANA LIGHT

# DREAM TIME TABLE

THIS LOVELY HAND-PAINTED TABLE CAN SIT NEXT TO YOUR BED TO INSPIRE SWEET DREAMS. PERFECT FOR HOLDING YOUR PAINTED DECANTER AND A DRINKING GLASS ON TOP, THE TABLE ALSO HAS A HANDY DRAWER WITH A MOON-SHAPED KNOB FOR KEEPING A JOURNAL AND PEN TO RECORD YOUR DREAMS.

IF WE ARE TRAVELING HEAVENWARD,
WE ARE ALREADY IN HEAVEN.

*William Temple*

Archbishop of Canterbury

BE EMPTY. BE STILL. WATCH EVERY-
THING JUST COME AND GO.
EMERGING FROM THE SOURCE.
RETURNING TO THE SOURCE. THIS
IS THE WAY OF NATURE.

*Lao Tzu*
Chinese founder of Taoism

## MATERIALS

Light-colored nightstand

Newspaper

Silver spray enamel

Self-adhesive paper

Spray enamel in two shades of blue

Spray enamel in two shades of purple

Clear spray enamel

Silver-colored drawer pull with moon motif

## TOOLS

Screwdriver

Pencil

Scissors or craft knife

Masking tape

## INSTRUCTIONS

### 1.

Use the screwdriver to remove the original drawer pull from the nightstand.

### 2.

Be sure to work outside or in a well-ventilated space. Protect your work area with newspaper, and spray the entire nightstand with silver paint. Allow to dry.

### 3.

Draw a spiral and 55 star shapes in two sizes on the self-adhesive paper (you may wish to use stencils). Cut them out. Using the photo as a guide, adhere the shapes to the table.

### 4.

Using one shade of blue paint, spray the top of each side of the table. Below that, spray a band of the other shade of blue. Below it, spray a band of the lighter shade of purple. Spray the shelf and bottom of each side in dark purple. Allow to dry.

### 5.

Peel up the self-adhesive paper spiral. Spray the silver design very lightly with both shades of purple to speckle the surface. Peel up the self-adhesive paper stars.

### 6.

Wrap the bottom of the table in newspaper, using the masking tape to secure it. Spray the top of the table with light-purple paint. Allow to dry.

### 7.

Spray the entire table with clear enamel. Allow to dry, then attach the drawer pull with a moon motif.

*Designer:* JANE DAVIS

# GENTLE SLEEP SACHETS

SIMPLE TO MAKE, THESE LITTLE PILLOWS CONTAIN SOOTHING HERBS TO HELP YOU SLEEP. YOU ONLY USE A SMALL AMOUNT OF HERBS. UNLIKE MOST SACHETS OR POTPOURRIS, THESE PILLOWS ARE NOT MEANT TO BE STRONG SMELLING, BUT RATHER TO HINT AT THE FRAGRANCE THEY CONTAIN, SUBTLY SCENTING YOUR DREAMS.

SO I KNOW THAT IT IS A GOOD THING I AM GOING TO DO; AND BECAUSE NO GOOD THING CAN BE DONE BY ANY PERSON ALONE; I WILL FIRST MAKE AN OFFERING AND SEND A VOICE TO THE SPIRIT OF THE WORLD, THAT IT MAY HELP ME BE TRUE.

*Black Elk*

Oglala Sioux holy man and seer

## MATERIALS
### (FOR EACH PILLOW)

Thin batting, 14 x 14 inches

Fleece fabric, 18 x 18 inches (46 x 46 cm)

Dried herbs

Six-strand embroidery floss

Decorative buttons for closing blanket stitch pillow

## TOOLS

Embroidery needle

Sewing needle and thread

## INSTRUCTIONS

NOTE: *The batting insert is the same for each pillow. Place a small amount of the herbs in the center of the batting, and fold two sides of the batting over the herbs, then fold the other two sides over the first, adjusting the finished size to a square or rectangle of the desired finished pillow size.*

### PILLOW WITH PULL-THROUGH CLOSURE

#### 1.

With the fleece wrong side up, place the filled and folded batting in the center of the fleece, diagonally.

Fold two opposite sides of the fleece into the center, overlapping the batting.

#### 2.

Cut a slit in one corner of the fleece, diagonal to the sides of the fleece, approximately $1^1/2$ inches (4 cm) long and 2 inches (5 cm) from the point. Pull the opposite end of the fleece through the slit until the fleece is pulled into a square or rectangle.

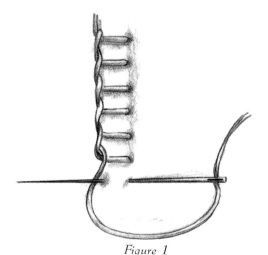

*Figure 1*

## BLANKET STITCH POCKET PILLOW

### 1.

Cut the fleece into a rectangle 18 x 7 inches (46 x 18 cm). Fold the bottom up 7 inches, so the fleece is now 7 x 11 inches (18 x 28 cm).

### 2.

Attach a 24-inch (61 cm) length of six—strand embroidery floss to the top left corner of the folded fabric. Blanket stitch around the edge of the folded fleece, working through both layers, attaching the sides of the bag together. To blanket stitch, work from left to right, bringing the needle from the back to the front. Insert the needle from front to back to front in a single motion. Before pulling the needle through the fabric, carry the floss under the point of the needle, as shown in figure 1. The stitch length can be alternated to add a pattern effect to the finishing edge. Continue blanket stitching along the bottom edge and up the other side, and around the single layer of fleece until you reach the beginning of your stitching. Hide the tails of floss inside the bag.

### 3.

Slide the herb-filled batting inside the fleece bag. Fold down the top flap of the bag. Sew a decorative button to the front of the flap and the front of the bag. Attach three 8-inch (20.5 cm) lengths of floss to the base of the decorative button on the flap. Braid the floss until it is long enough to loop around the other decorative button, and attach the tail ends to the base of the button on the flap.

## DESIGNER NOTE:

Many herbs have healing properties and are believed to also have spiritual ones. Here are a few you might choose for your sleep sachet, along with some of the beneficial qualities associated with them:

**Lavender:** relieves headaches

**Chamomile:** relaxes, helps you sleep

**Rosemary:** helps you remember dreams

**Dill:** encourages sleep

**Mugwort:** brings vivid dreams

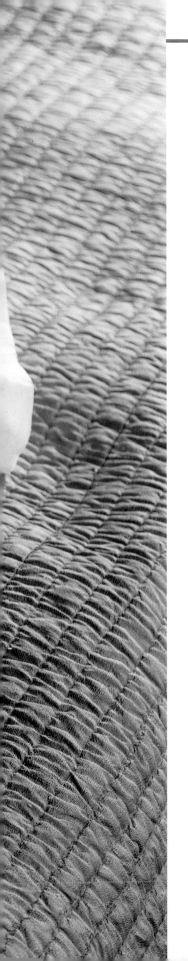

*Designer:* DIANA LIGHT

# DREAM CATCHER PILLOWCASE

ON YOUR PILLOWCASE, EMBROIDER SYMBOLS REPRESENTING THE FOUR ELEMENTS TO HARNESS THEIR ENERGY AND HELP YOU CAPTURE POWERFUL DREAMS.

HEAR ME, FOUR QUARTERS OF THE WORLD—A RELATIVE I AM! GIVE ME THE STRENGTH TO WALK THE SOFT EARTH, A RELATIVE TO ALL THAT IS! GIVE ME THE EYES TO SEE AND THE STRENGTH TO UNDERSTAND, THAT I MAY BE LIKE YOU. WITH YOUR POWER ONLY CAN I FACE THE WINDS.

*Black Elk*

Oglala Sioux holy man and seer

## MATERIALS

Symbols sized to 2-inch (5 cm) squares (below)

Transfer paper for fabric

Pillowcase

4 colors of embroidery floss

## TOOLS

Scissors

Straight pins or masking tape

Ballpoint pen

Embroidery hoop

Embroidery needle

Tape measure

## INSTRUCTIONS

### 1.

Cut out the symbols, leaving a $^1/_4$-inch (6 mm) border. Evenly space them along the edge of the pillowcase, pinning or taping them to the fabric.

### 2.

Use transfer paper and pen to transfer the symbols and squares to the pillowcase.

### 3.

Mount the pillowcase in the embroidery hoop. Separate the floss into three-strand pieces, and use a chain stitch to embroider the symbols. To chain stitch, bring the needle up from the bottom, then back down through the same hole. Pull the thread through, leaving a small loop. Bring the needle up a stitch in front of the loop, and then through it. Pull tightly, and repeat. (See page 115.)

### 4.

Use thread of contrasting color to backstitch the square outlines. To backstitch, take a stitch, then bring the needle back up through the fabric two stitches back. Repeat.

SKIP WADE

SPIRIT REACHES IN FOUR DIRECTIONS,
FLOWS NOW THIS WAY, NOW THAT.
IT PENETRATES EVERYWHERE
AND EVERYTHING.
ABOVE, IT BRUSHES THE SKIES.
BELOW, IT SURROUNDS THE EARTH.
IT TRANSFORMS AND NOURISHES THE
TEN THOUSAND THINGS.

*Chang-Tzu*
Taoist pantheist

# Contributing Designers

JUDI ASHE lives in Black Mountain, North Carolina. Committed to the premise that art can be a healing tool, she conducts workshops in making clay objects and creates items for spiritual healing work, as well as other functional pieces, and sculptural work for galleries around the country. "Clay has a memory," she says. "It is of this earth and all that has occurred over time. I have worked with many materials over the years and only clay has had such a profound grounding and healing effect on me."

ANNE ASHLEY of Louisville, Kentucky, is handy with both scissors and paintbrush. She works in several media including clay, foam-board sculpture, mosaic, paper, and fabric. She describes her art as her spiritual practice and says her philosophy is best summed up by the words of Van Morrison, who sang: "Enlightenment don't know what it is."

GABE CYR says, "I have discarded the notion that I need to know what I want to be when I grow up in favor of deciding that it is the journey and not the goal that is the focus of my life." On that journey she describes herself as "a soul who teaches, creates, helps people explore the wise messages they want to give themselves, but haven't quite heard yet—all with art." The works she creates include altered books, dolls, and fabric objects. Her work has been exhibited in several galleries and books, and she lives in Asheville, North Carolina.

JANE DAVIS is an author, teacher, and designer of fine arts and crafts. Her books include *Knitting with Beads* (Lark, 2003), and her projects have been featured in numerous magazines. "I believe that working on any type of creative outlet is an important and necessary part of a person's health and well being," she says. "In beadwork, the repetitiveness of the stitching is like dance steps or a song: it's just fun to do. To get a beautiful finished project in the end is a wonderful bonus, but I find the process is what enriches the most."

VALENTIN GOMEZ lives in Mexico and Abingdon, Virginia. His favorite achievements in art have been taking abandoned or broken objects and redesigning them to make something new. He is currently working on a series of giant insects made of fence posts, tin, and barbed wire.

FRANCOISE HESSELINK, L.Ac., studied the oriental healing arts in Japan and has been practicing acupuncture for over 20 years, currently in Asheville, North Carolina. In the course of her practice and her own healing journey, she discovered the importance of the spiritual as the root of all true healing. "Essential oils are a great and fun help in connecting with your spiritual center," she says. "They have been used in that way for thousands of years in many parts of the world."

DIANA LIGHT creates beautiful objects and spreads good energy in Asheville, North Carolina. Skilled in many media, including needlework, glass painting, and design, she says the common thread in all her work "is the inspiration I find in nature. The natural world is also where I get a lot of strength and comfort for dealing with life." She is the author of a forthcoming Lark Book on batik.

MARY JANE MILLER has explored a variety of spiritual art forms, including painting retablos, for some 20 years. "I am particularly fascinated by what transpires when a human uses prayer as a solution to life's frustrations and desires," she says. Currently her work has focused on Russian iconography. She lives in Abingdon, Virginia, and Mexico.

LISA SARASOHN designs belly-celebrating accessories as part of "Honoring Your Belly," a program she has created that encourages women to experience the body's center as sacred, not shameful. Based in Asheville, North Carolina, the program uses various forms of creative expression as well as power-centering movement and breathing exercises drawn from yoga and other healing arts. For more information, visit www.honoringyourbelly.com.

ELISHA SIGLE, of Floyd, Virginia, began making meditation cushions after attending a Buddhist retreat. A beader, she was inspired to add the *om* symbol to her work. "I think it's like folding origami cranes," she said. "I *om* while I bead, and perhaps after 10,000 of them, my wish for enlightenment will come true." Her work can be viewed and purchased at www.shamvara.com.

TERRY TAYLOR is a multi-talented artist whose work includes jewelry design, lamp making, egg decorating, gilding, and the pique-assiette mosaic technique. His work often incorporates *milagros* or other spiritual items and imagery. He lives in Asheville, North Carolina.

NICOLE TUGGLE is a mixed-media artist whose recent work has focused on collage and assemblage constructions. She finds beauty in found objects and old, neglected treasures. Check out more of her work at www.sigilation.com. She lives in Asheville, North Carolina.

LUANN UDELL is an award-winning, nationally exhibited mixed media artist who works from her renovated barn studio in Keene, New Hampshire. Her work is sold in fine galleries and craft stores across the country, she is the author of *Weekend Crafter: Rubber Stamp Carving* (Lark, 2003). Her artwork is inspired by the prehistoric cave paintings of Lascaux, France. She creates textile collages, polymer sculpture, and jewelry resembling ancient artifacts—remnants of a lost culture, an imagined prehistory. See her work at www.durable-goods.com

Contributing photographer JON BOWER is also a full-time environmental scientist presently based in the UK. His cameras always go with him to whatever weird and wonderful places he is visiting for business or pleasure. Select images from Jon's archive of exotic portraiture, abstract, urban, environmental, landscape and lifestyle images can be seen at www.apexphotos.com. His work appears in many books and magazines world-wide, and is featured here on pages 7, 9, 17, 39, 51, 67, 79, and 99.

# Index